The Day
I Almost
Destroyed the
Boston Symphony
and Other Stories

by
John Sant'Ambrogio

Nebbadoon Press

Santa Barbara

The Day I Almost Destroyed
the Boston Symphony
and Other Stories

© 2010 John Sant'Ambrogio

Nebbadoon Press

800 500-9086

www.NebbadoonPress.com

ISBN 978-1-891331-15-2

Printed in the U.S.A.

Cover photo by Ken Lee
Back cover photo by Dan Dreyfus
Cover design by Gary S. Albright

Dedicated to my children

Stephanie
Sara
Michael

and my grandchildren

Bella
Brie
Sebastian

Before I made symphonic music performance my lifework, I always thought of this noble and sublime occupation as being devoid of humor. After all, classical music is often called serious music. I should have known better.

o   o   o

A symphony orchestra is a metaphor for life.

John Sant'Ambrogio

March 2010
Steamboat Springs, CO

This memoir is based on what I remember happening in my musical career, and any inconsistencies or oversights, condensing of time, and/or change in actual dialogue is due to the span of years between these covers. – J.S.A.

Table of Contents

CHAPTER

1

MY MUSICAL CRIME

When my father took me to my first symphony concert in the late forties, I was surprised by how much I actually enjoyed the whole experience. I was in my early teens, and though curious to hear this famous Boston Symphony Orchestra that my dad had been raving about, I had not expected to like the concert very much. After all, growing up with two musicians for parents, I had been hearing piano and violin music twenty-four hours a day since I was born. What could be so different about symphonic music? I had just begun to study the cello at the time, but I really was not yet interested in classical music. It was all right, I guess, but did we have to hear so much of it? Sometimes my close association with it even made me feel a little awkward. Nobody else I knew had both a mother and a father who played and taught music to earn a living, and this made me different. When I was with my friends I kept quiet about all the serious music that was going on in my house. They didn't want to hear about it anyway. They were into sports and popular music. When I was back in the house with my parents, I quietly rebelled against that "long-hair stuff," and that was not easy without siblings for allies.

Besides all the live music I was hearing every day, my father would often play some old 78s from a large collection he had amassed over the years. A few of those recordings were of performances by the BSO under Serge Koussevitzky, and they were my favorites. But those records never sounded anything like what I found myself listening to at my first live orchestra concert. All of a sudden, music took on another dimension. The depth of the sound of the different string sections, often playing in unison, gave me chills. Symphonic music was different. That concert opened my ears to beauty I had never heard before.

In 1949, about a year or two after my first live orchestra concert, my parents started a small summer music school called Red Fox Music Camp near Tanglewood, Massachusetts, the summer home of the Boston Symphony. This happy turn of events gave me a great opportunity to continue my love affair with the BSO and to study the face of every musician in that orchestra. Those were the summers when I couldn't wait for the weekends to come: Our music camp would pack into a bus and make the hour trip to Tanglewood to hear the Symphony's

Saturday-morning open rehearsals. We would race into the Shed, the symphony's summer concert hall, along with 5,000 other music lovers, trying to grab the best seats closest to the stage. This huge structure resembled a giant airplane hangar much more than it did a concert hall. Its dirt floor and stark metal chairs might have seemed out of place when the musicians later donned their white jackets for the evening performances, but it was all pretty glamorous to me. I guess I was impressed by the great size of the shed, the large audience, and all the excitement there was in the air as the musicians began to come onstage.

The expansive, lush green lawns and the towering two-hundred-year-old elms on the Tanglewood grounds were all included in the 360-degree view we could see from our seats if we were to let our eyes wander from the source of the music making. Yet, with all that natural beauty so close by, we still focused all our attention on those one hundred men and one woman who would soon sit on the broad, brightly-lit stage—glamour personified. Someday I, too, had to be on that stage with everyone looking at me, for as a teenager, music was merely a close second to glamour.

Once we were settled in our seats on those misty Saturday mornings, we became deeply engrossed in our favorite pastime, orchestra-watching.

"Look, here comes Joe de Pasquale. Doesn't he look scary, so serious like he could be a Mafia boss? Just wait till you see how great he is at leading his viola section. There's Richard Burgin, the concertmaster. Watch his right foot when he plays. It will rock back and forth in time to the music. They say he's always thinking about the card game he's just played offstage, so he never looks like he knows where he is until the conductor gives the first beat. See that violinist on the last stand of the second violins? He's one of the best players in the orchestra, and they say someday he may get to be the concertmaster."

All of our chatter was part of the fun because we enjoyed what we saw almost as much as what we were about to hear. When the music began, it was glorious. I can still remember the first two pieces I heard the BSO perform in the Shed at Tanglewood: Brahms' *Variations on a Theme by Haydn* and Handel's *Water Music*. I can't play them today without reliving that special part of my life when I enjoyed long happy summers in beautiful New England.

But this orchestra that we watched and listened to so intently during my first season as a Red Fox camper would be the same one I would "destroy" some ten years later. It would be as if I had opened the doors leading onto the stage and hurled a bomb right into the midst of this great ensemble. I would completely demolish them.

4

When this embarrassing experience occurred, I had just recently become one of them, and that was what made it so painful.

This disaster happened sometime during my second or third year with the BSO. Until this event, my time with the BSO had been joyful. Since it had long been a dream of mine to become a member of that orchestra's cello section, those first years were the fruit of all my labor. Midway through this particular season, the personnel manager called me into his office to tell me that I had been selected to play in a little offstage band (two violins and one cello) that would be heard in the final moments of Berlioz's *Harold in Italy*. This work featured our principal violist, Joe de Pasquale, as the soloist. The three of us had been selected because we sat far back in the orchestra near the doors by the side of the stage. Our conductor felt it would be convenient for us to slip off the stage discreetly at just the right moment in the music and play our part offstage without disturbing the audience.

I was very excited because I knew this could be my big moment, a chance to show off. Finally all my colleagues were going to hear my beautiful sound. Although only two or three notes of the forty or so that I was to play with the little ensemble were actually solo, and these did not occur until late in our contribution, I was sure that everyone would be able to hear them. Now all my colleagues would know why I had been selected to be one of their newest members. I would surely impress them with my decisiveness and poise. For a brief moment, I would be out of the shadows, not just a section player, or to be more accurate, last-chair section player, but a soloist. I was determined to make the best of those few notes and send them soaring above the orchestra. My concept of how to play that music was probably not what Berlioz had in mind when he wrote it, but I'm sure that he would have forgiven me had he known how much I wanted to impress my fellow musicians.

All week the rehearsals went well. My colleagues actually complimented me, and I was looking forward to the concert. The first performance got off to a good start, and soon we were nearing the conclusion of the Berlioz and the moment when our little band was to "do its stuff." By a prearranged signal, my two partners and I sneaked off the stage and assembled with our stands and chairs behind one of the closed stage doors. We could hear Joe and the orchestra playing beautifully, and we prepared ourselves to perform our small part in this exciting concert. The house was packed, and I was hoping an additional million or so were listening to the live broadcast. I wanted them all to hear what I expected to be the beautiful sounds of my cello.

Our moment came. The stagehands opened the doors to reveal us, and we started to play. The rest of the orchestra grew quiet as was indicated in the score by the composer. At first our maestro had a pleasant expression on his face as he turned and gracefully waved his long baton at us, playing through the open doors offstage. This was really getting exciting, and I was proud to be sitting there making music with such a great orchestra. The best part was that, in a few seconds, I was going to play those solo notes that I had worked so hard to prepare. Though I was staring intently at my music at the time, I was aware of a lot more than just the notes on the page. I was relishing the whole picture. I saw the backs of my colleagues' heads on the stage in front of me, and I could even see the audience up in the side balcony. They were all concentrating on the quiet, dreamlike music that we were setting adrift out into our beautiful concert hall. This peaceful mood that we were creating was intended by the composer to be a short interlude just before the rest of the orchestra and the viola soloist were to rejoin us to bring the last movement of the Berlioz symphonic work to a rousing conclusion. Unfortunately our peaceful mood didn't last long because almost immediately after our entrance something quite unexpected happened.

Charles Münch, our conductor, one of the world's most brilliant interpreters of French music, was occasionally a little confusing to follow. This, unfortunately, became one of those occasions. All of a sudden my colleagues and I couldn't agree about where our director was. It was a struggle for us to follow him and still stay together. This was not the way we had done it during the rehearsals; we were breaking new ground.

Then I could not believe my eyes. Münch, now with a scowl on his face, was gesturing wildly towards us and indicating what to me looked like a downbeat, which was also the signal for my solo entrance. But by my calculations, I still had one beat to go. With a quarter of a second to make one of the most important decisions of my career, I hesitated for just an instant: "I think we're missing a beat here somewhere, but how do we ignore the conductor?" I threw caution to the wind and a very precious beat out the window; I did what I thought my maestro wanted me to do. I dug into that cello with all my might and started playing with a sound so large that I'm sure even those in the last seats in the top balcony could hear me clearly.

Almost immediately I began having second thoughts about my decision to charge ahead. I had a nagging suspicion that I had indeed entered one beat too soon, and I was already receiving clues to that effect from center stage.

But it was too late to go back and start again. Instead, I plowed ahead with an unrelenting tone. All the time I knew that, if my suspicions were correct, the early entrance and my insistence on finishing what I had begun would soon destroy the Boston Symphony Orchestra.

What happened next was like watching film footage of an old skyscraper being blown up. In slow motion you see the once magnificent structure slowly crumble to earth in a cloud of dust. Mr. de Pasquale, still playing his viola beautifully, continued to follow the conductor as I guess he should have, but my early entrance confused the string sections. Some went with the soloist, and the rest went with me, wailing away offstage.

Then the woodwinds apparently couldn't decide which half of the string section they should go with, and soon they, too, were going in different directions. The brass needed to hear a solid woodwind section to keep their place, and since one was not available, they were a ship without a rudder, heading for the rocks. The entire orchestra gradually descended into an abyss, all because I had entered one beat too soon. I had become a giant wrecking ball to the Boston Symphony.

Through it all I never stopped playing. As I finished the last note of my contribution, the stagehands began closing the doors on the chaos out in the hall. There was only a brief moment between the last note of my solo and the final sealing of those old wooden doors, but it was more than enough time for me to assess what I had just done. The last glimpse I had of Münch, as the big stage doors closed, showed a desperate man. No longer smiling or even scowling, his face showed terror as he flailed his arms at his once magnificent orchestra in a futile attempt to restore order. It was hopeless. Our magnificent Symphony was fast crumbling at his feet. It went from Berlioz to a general free-for-all in ten seconds flat.

Our little offstage band was now finished, but we did not move. We were stunned. What had we done, or more to the point, what had I done? We could hear horrible noises coming from the other side of the door, but there was nothing we could do to help our comrades. That time had passed, and now I knew my earlier suspicions had been correct.

I also knew I was in deep trouble.

CHAPTER

2

BLESSED ARE THE MERCIFUL

How the Boston Symphony ever put itself back together again at the end of that memorable Friday-afternoon concert is still a mystery to me. Perhaps it was our principal trumpeter, Roger Voisin, blasting out some motif familiar to all, who rallied the musicians and enabled them to finally join forces at the finish. Maybe everyone scrambled to join the loudest and most brilliant voice in the orchestra, and the one, by its commanding presence, that had the best chance of herding the confused musicians toward the final chord. Whatever it was, it must have been a miracle, because nothing else could have put all the parts of the BSO back together again after the damage I had done to it that Friday afternoon. I don't believe there is a person alive today who remembers exactly who did what and when to save the BSO. The whole incident was best forgotten, and everyone was just grateful that most of the musicians eventually stopped playing at the same time.

After some polite applause, the soloist and the maestro made their exit from the stage through the same doors behind which our little trio now waited, those doors to which we kept our ears pinned as we had prayed for our colleagues to salvage the mess that I had created. Still in shock, we were barely able to get out of the way of those two unhappy men. Joe de Pasquale, the one musician most affected by my mistake, just looked at me and said, "Oh, John!" Münch was so angry that he did not look at me. I should have fled to South America immediately, but the horror of what I had done paralyzed me. The rest of the orchestra began pouring off the stage, almost trampling me, and there was not one consoling face among them. Everyone was having a wonderful time enjoying a disaster for which they were not responsible. "Great job, John," was repeated over and over, followed by laughter.

Soon everyone was gone, and I was standing there alone by the stage door holding my cello, not sure of my next move. The thought came to me to try to apologize to the maestro. This was probably a foolish idea. Todd Perry, the orchestra's manager, who was guarding the maestro's dressing-room door, kindly listened to my request to see Münch and then quickly left to speak with him. Fortunately I was spared the immediate pain of a face-to-face meeting. Loud screams soon began emanating from Münch's room, and Todd quickly returned to tell me that this was not the best time for a reconciliation.

Still in shock, I went down to the men's locker room to find my cello case and pack up my instrument. Mercifully there seemed to be no one left in the building. That was fine because, by now, my embarrassment about what I had done had become acute, and I didn't want to see a soul. After lugging my now heavy cello to my car, I drove home and told my wife to pack our bags. "Peg, I just destroyed the BSO."

My wife, who never panicked at my panics, said, without looking up from what she was doing, "Don't worry. Everything will be all right." This did not help much. I couldn't sleep that night as I replayed the horrible moment over and over again, hoping that it was all a bad dream, which of course it wasn't.

The next evening our little trio decided to get together in a dressing room before the second concert to rehearse our few notes and see if we could figure out how to prevent another disaster. Since most of what we had to play was composed of half notes and quarter notes, we were a little puzzled at how I could have become so confused in the first place. I think we decided that no matter what Münch did in this next performance, we were going to stick together, not strike out on our own as I had done the day before.

Just before the concert was to begin, we stopped practicing and rushed to get onstage before the downbeat. As I was walking through the narrow backstage area, I saw that Münch was sitting a few feet from where I had to pass to enter the stage. He often relaxed at this spot just before making his long walk to the podium, and this I should have remembered. Since he had not yet seen me, I seriously considered spinning around on my heels to enter the stage from the other side. In a few seconds, I could tell that he could see me too.

Immediately his countenance took on a frightening appearance. As I drew abreast of him, I could sense that the end was near. There would be no tomorrow for me, at least with the BSO. Münch had a reputation for firing new players with whom he was not one hundred percent happy, and I could see how I might easily fit into that category. I turned my head slightly to catch one last glimpse of my executioner before the blade fell, and then he did something unexpected. He laughed. Maybe it was only a chuckle, but it was the most compassionate sound I had ever heard. It was as if the heavens opened, and I had been taken up in a golden chariot. Alleluia! I loved him.

That night, when the stage doors opened and it was time for our "merry little band" to play, we saw a smiling conductor facing us, giving us a beat so clear that a first-year Suzuki student could have followed it. Münch was taking no chances and was not going to mess with a live cannon on deck. The BSO took that Berlioz *Harold* all over the East Coast on tour, stopping, I believe, in Hartford, New Haven, and New York. Münch always smiled and got clearer and clearer at each performance until he was practically playing our instruments for us.

I cherish the memory of that man. Without saying a word, he let us know that he also took some responsibility for what had happened at that fateful concert. Because of my inexperience at the time, I didn't know that Münch's upbeats could often look like downbeats, especially when he became frustrated with what he thought were inattentive players. It usually took a new player a year to figure this out, and by the next season I, too, would be gleefully watching the latest rookie fall for the famous Münch downbeat/upbeat gambit. The maestro kindly took all this into account. This was unusual because kindness was not something one could always expect from a conductor. By the end of the tour, our little ensemble was sounding pretty good, and it was again a thrill for me to be making great music with those exciting artists. We never disturbed the beautiful playing of Joe de Pasquale again, and more important, I was never fired.

That was the good news. The bad news was that the BSO would not be the last great orchestra I would bring to a grinding halt.

CHAPTER

3

NICE WORK IF YOU CAN GET IT

It's been almost fifty years since that debacle in Boston—nine playing in the BSO, thirty-seven as the principal cellist in the Saint Louis Symphony, and five in retirement. Most of the time I'm not as dangerous to have around as I was that Friday afternoon in Boston's Symphony Hall. That disaster and a few others I will soon relate were the exceptions, I hope, to my usual, ahem, flawless music making. Exceptions are always more fun to tell about than the rule, and they improve with age. Besides, those exceptions only make us appreciate the perfect performance that much more. Who wants to hear about our successes anyway? That's what's expected of us. But those flaws make everything else seem good by comparison. They also remind us that, though we may be performing what many feel is God-inspired, we are only human ourselves. Looking back on my life, I see that I was as human as the next man. Still, with all the little imperfections I have observed and the occasional embarrassment that I may have experienced over the past fifty years as a professional symphony musician, there is no other field of endeavor that I would rather have explored. What could have been more fun than making music in two of our country's greatest orchestras?

Consider this: If you like music, once you join us, you will certainly get a seat close to the action. In fact, if you like, you can have this seat placed exactly where you want (within reason) by our always helpful stage managers. Besides, your music makes people feel happy and relaxed, unlike a visit to the dentist or an IRS auditor.

If you like traveling, it is a great way to see the world at someone else's expense. You may have to play a concert at night, but what a great way to break up the sightseeing. You can spend your mornings in cathedrals and your afternoons in castles. In the evening you can play a little "night music" followed by coffee and Viennese pastry at a charming café. Since the symphony orchestra management takes care of everything on tour, you don't have to worry about airline tickets, baggage, or hotels. You can get a little spoiled by all this attention, however, as I found out on my first trip abroad without the orchestra. I missed a plane connection in England because I forgot that the orchestra personnel manager was not there to push me aboard.

Times have changed recently, meaning things are a little tougher than they were in my day. Orchestras are not touring or recording as much. Salaries are stabilizing and in some cases decreasing. One hopes that these hard times won't last forever, but in the year 2010, in the top twenty orchestras in the United States, the minimum pay ranges are now somewhere between a low of $40,000 a year to a high of $125,000. Health care is most often provided, and the on-the-job workload is eighteen to thirty hours per week, with usually an additional fifteen to twenty hours of "homework." At the time of my retirement in 2005, these orchestras offered four to eight paid vacation weeks per year. Not bad! What is so important is that, in each of these individual orchestras of one hundred musicians, there is often less discrimination regarding race, gender, sexual orientation, age, or other distinguishing human characteristics than in the rest of society. Sounds pretty good to me. It makes sense that everyone is rushing to join.

Though not all musicians see an orchestra life as their ideal, today we are seeing a flood of incredibly talented young people who are paying good money to fly all over the country to audition against hundreds of other musicians. Often this is for just one opening for their particular instrument in each orchestra. Applications for one string position can range from sixty to three hundred, and that's often after the applicants have been screened.

With the winds, brass, and percussion—and don't even mention the harp—it is even more competitive. One major orchestra, I am told, considered one thousand applicants for a trumpet position. You can get better odds in Las Vegas. Because there are so many talented players for orchestras to choose from today, when you attend a symphony concert you are hearing the *crème de la crème*. This is true even in the smaller, less financially stable organizations.

Things have changed dramatically since I first started my career. In 1959, for one cello vacancy, I found myself competing against only seven other players. As recently as 2005, when I was the chairman of the cello audition committee for the Saint Louis Symphony, I would have often heard, over a period of five weeks, more than one hundred wonderful musicians, who were competing for one or two openings in the cello section.

Fifty years ago, it was frequently a matter of who you knew and where you went to school that opened the audition doors. Today, openings are always posted in our national musicians' union magazine. Back then, the all-powerful conductor could be ten feet away from you as you played, and he could decide whether he liked your hair style as much as your musicianship. This same conductor often could and would choose who he wanted to have in his orchestra without consulting anyone else. Now a lot more of us get into the act. A committee of nine or ten symphony musicians, selected by secret ballot by their colleagues, sits behind a large screen to judge contestants during the audition. This prevents us from recognizing our friends, helping us to make impartial decisions. We even put carpet on the floor so we cannot tell by the sound of their footsteps whether the auditionees are male or female. When the conductor does join the audition committee during the finals, he or she has one vote and rarely makes the all-important decision alone.

In addition to this traditional route of auditioning for orchestra positions, at which it is so hard to succeed because of the odds, young musicians must now consider alternative music-making positions such as teaching younger musicians and performing in smaller communities. This is a growth industry: small-venue concert series set by the musicians themselves, which in turn build new audiences that may include the students' extended families and friends.

Here I should pay tribute to our former conductor Leonard Slatkin, who is often credited with building the Saint Louis Symphony into the great orchestra it is today. One of the most important things he did was to show his faith in the audition process by never overruling the audition committee and by constantly seeking our opinions. This confidence that he had in the audition committee permeated the entire symphony, and over the years there developed a great appreciation for collegiality. The willingness of a particular candidate to be a team player was as important to the audition committee as his or her brilliance on the instrument. A fair and wise audition committee is one of the most important factors in molding the character and raising the morale of an orchestra. It can be the soul of the institution. I'm firmly convinced that the Saint Louis Symphony is one of the greatest orchestras in the country because of its audition process.

I'm reminded of an occasion many years ago when a former music director of ours talked to a musician who was a judge on the audition committee during a particular candidate's performance. Although I didn't think it was intentional, it seemed to me that the conductor could have influenced the musician's vote, and I expressed my concern. I was promptly asked by the conductor to leave the audition committee, and he didn't speak to me for a year. Just one year later a clause was added to our symphony contract that forbade any talking between members of the audition committee, including the conductor, until after a candidate had finished his or her performance and the members of the committee had taken one secret ballot. I was invited back onto the committee at about the same time, and we have been following the contract ever since. The conductor and I renewed our friendship, and he graciously ignored my big mouth.

One might ask, "How did they, back in those bad old days, ever have good orchestras when the selection process was sometimes based on the dictatorial powers of a mighty maestro and a little dash of old-fashioned politics"? Well, they did. Many of us in the music world heard that the Philadelphia Orchestra used to be somewhat political in its recruiting, and it was. Yet it is still recognized as one of the greatest orchestras in the world. Many of its musicians knew not only who were the best up-and-coming music students in the leading conservatories, but also who the best team players were. This information went to their illustrious music director Eugene Ormandy, who had the power to install whomever he wished. The Curtis Institute of Music in Philadelphia in particular was a wonderful garden for Ormandy, where some of the most talented young musicians in the country were groomed by members of his orchestra to fit into their system. Sounds pretty smart to me.

So which way is better? Without question, the present system, which provides safeguards to ensure fairness. It also makes it possible for orchestras to have a myriad of applicants from which to choose. I'm glad that I am not looking for a job today. As it was, I felt it was a miracle that I was invited to join the BSO in 1959, but this may be the way that everyone who successfully runs the gauntlet to enter the exclusive world of a great symphony orchestra feels.

CHAPTER

4

FRIENDLY GLADIATORS

The proverbial "they" often say that if something good is supposed to happen to you, no matter how much you try, you can't prevent it from occurring; thus you should relax and enjoy the ride. I'm not sure I always believed that, but perhaps I should.

As I was getting close to finishing graduate school, I was still without any job prospects for the coming year. Having plugged myself into the "system," I was asking friends and teachers to arrange private auditions for me with the great maestros like Eugene Ormandy and George Szell. This is something that would be impossible today. At that time there were not so many union regulations to stop conductors from doing anything they wanted to do. There were also far fewer qualified musicians to choose from, and in 1959 conductors didn't seem to mind taking the time to hear single candidates for their orchestras if someone they respected asked them to. One

Saturday morning, Szell spent forty-five minutes sitting alone in Cleveland's darkened Severance Hall listening to just one cellist, me, play.

Even though Szell asked me to come back and play for him again, he didn't give me the job, which really depressed me. I was so upset that I forgot to take my sheet music, marked with my name, Sant'Ambrogio, with me when I left. (Thirty-five years later my daughter Sara was soloing with the Cleveland Orchestra. The manager came up to her and asked her if the sheet music that they had saved for all those years was hers because it was marked Sant'Ambrogio.)

After some long car trips from Athens, Ohio, to Cleveland and Columbus to play scary solo performances for these two great conductors, Szell and Ormandy, I seemed no closer to entering their orchestras (Cleveland and Philadelphia, respectively) than when I had first picked up the cello eleven years earlier. I was hearing a lot of maybes: "Maybe you should go home and practice scales and play for me again in a month," or "Maybe you should look into a different cello, and by the way, you didn't hold that note long enough," or "Maybe you should come to the general audition in the fall because maybe then you can win a seat in my orchestra." What I wanted to hear was, "Young man, our orchestra will not be complete until you join our ranks."

Obviously, being the best cellist in my college orchestra did not impress the big leagues.

A high-school string teaching position, offered to me just before I was to finish graduate school at Ohio University, seemed to be the only way I was going to make a living and still be in music. I had already taught one year in the public schools and loved it, but I wanted to try something different. Hoping that maybe a cello position in some little orchestra would open up in the near future, I turned down the high-school job and left Ohio University with no real job prospects in sight for the next year. I headed off with my wife, Peg, to be boys' counselor and cello teacher for the tenth season at our family's summer music camp in the Berkshires. Here is where that "something good" began to happen, and no matter how hard I tried to stop it, I couldn't.

One afternoon while I was high up on a ladder doing some last minute painting on a big barn, Mrs. Goldberg, a parent of a newly arriving student from Boston, shouted up to me, "Mr. S, did you hear about that last-minute audition the Boston Symphony Orchestra announced for a cello opening?" Incidentally, Mrs. Goldberg was in a trolley in Vienna twenty years earlier and was held down in her seat by a man sitting next to her when the Nazis came into the trolley car and demanded that all Jews stand up. Before her family was able to leave Austria, there was a knock at her door. When she opened it, there was a Nazi youth standing in front of her. He took one look at her and turned around and told his superior, "There are no Jews here." He knew her. I guess I should thank both of those brave souls for saving Mrs. Goldberg's life so that she was able to tell me about the audition.

I scrambled down the ladder, climbed into my 1949 Studebaker, and drove eighty miles per hour to Tanglewood to put my name on the audition list. I was put on the list. I was elated. The secretary at the BSO's Tanglewood office squeezed me in at the last minute. She probably put me on the list because there were only seven cellists able to come to the audition since the vacancy had just occurred in midseason, due to the death of a BSO cellist. Normally there could have been as many as two hundred talented cellists competing. The BSO was the orchestra I had always wanted to join. During the hour drive back to our camp, however, I had time to think about the impossible task ahead of me.

In those days a major part of all auditions was sight-reading. The conductors presented music to the applicants that supposedly none of them had seen before, to observe how well they could sight-read it. I was not yet a good sight-reader, but that wasn't the point. Usually no one was really sight-reading because everyone had practiced most of the orchestral literature for years at the best conservatories. That is, everyone but me. I had been able to squeeze in a lot of practicing on cello concerti and solo pieces while taking academic classes in college, but I didn't have time to do much with the orchestral literature. While my competitors had been familiarizing themselves with almost all the audition literature, it was almost certain that what they would give me to read would not look familiar.

The next day I took out a stack of orchestral studies and opened the first book to *Don Juan* by Richard Strauss. Just one piece took all afternoon to perfect. I could see that it was hopeless and I gave up.

There were easily fifty to one hundred or more major works I should learn, and there was not enough time even to scratch the surface. I thought, "Forget this audition. I'll wait for one when I have more time to prepare properly." The sun was out, so I went swimming with our campers. I was also the camp lifeguard and bus driver, so I had some justification to quit practicing. A good swim and a few other distractions pushed the audition to the back of my mind. At the end of the week my mother informed me that she had answered our camp's only phone when the BSO had called to confirm my audition the next morning. Not knowing that I had decided not to go, she had told them I would be there. Now I had to go, and I hadn't done anything all week to prepare. I was going to be humiliated.

The next morning as I began my drive over to the beautiful Tanglewood grounds, I half hoped that my car would break down, preventing me from getting there in time to compete and be embarrassed. Nothing went wrong on the trip over, and by the time I pulled into the parking lot outside the main Tanglewood gate, I was reasonably calm. The drive had given me time to do all the usual mental work that one does in these kinds of situations: "Just look at the big picture here, John. This is just one day in your life. It's not winning that counts, but how you play the game."

When I arrived all the other cellists had already begun to warm up in the backstage area. Everyone sounded great. Each was better than the next, and even the worst was better than I was. The most unsettling thing was that they all seemed happy to be there and were looking forward to the experience. Even though I, too, needed to warm up before the actual audition started, there was no way I was going to take out my cello and noodle around in front of those cellists, who all sounded like Pablo Casals. I immediately picked up my audition number and sneaked out the back door of the building into one of the beautiful public gardens near the theater. After making sure no one was around to hear me, I took my cello out and began warming up on the Saint Saëns *Cello Concerto*, which was the piece my friend Ling Tung said was the best piece to play at auditions. Thanks, Ling. Every so often, I peeked over the bushes to make sure I was still alone.

Because of the dead acoustics outdoors where I had been warming up, I had had to work hard at producing a big, pure tone. In the process I had become highly sensitive to exactly what was coming out of my instrument; thus, without realizing it, my cowardice started to pay off. When my number came up in the first round, and it was my turn to play my solo concerto on the stage, I was impressed with how full my cello sounded in the hall compared to the way it had in the garden.

This relaxed me some and, I think, helped me to play better than I normally would have. I was not that impressed, however, and when the BSO's personnel manager came backstage to announce the results of the first round, I didn't hold out much hope that I was still a contender. Surprisingly I was, but another cellist, whom I thought was terrific, had been eliminated. Since this was one of the first times that the BSO had used a screen for its auditions, I was sure they had mixed up the numbers and eliminated the wrong guy. The "wrong guy," several weeks later, went on to win the cello position in the Philadelphia Orchestra that I had originally wanted to fill. I found it interesting that the first player to be refused at our audition should immediately win a position in another prestigious orchestra. Mistake or not, I was still in the running.

But now something strange happened to me, like a basketball player who, for no earthly reason, begins to get "the touch" during a crucial game, and everything he throws up swishes through the rim, barely touching the net. I started to play better than I thought I could and unconsciously relaxed even more. Little by little, as the day wore on, more and more cellists were eliminated. I hardly noticed. It all seemed like a dream as I watched the whole process in amazement from someplace outside of myself.

Suddenly it was sight-reading time, and that woke me up. Walking out to the lone music stand in the middle of the darkened stage, I began to slip under the waves of fear. "Would you please read the music in front of you," said a voice in the auditorium where Charles Münch and a few principal players sat huddled together like a parole board reviewing a serial killer's unruly prison record. There were four difficult orchestral excerpts on the stand. I slowly checked each one and readied myself for the final humiliation.

Out of countless symphonies, overtures, and symphonic tone poems in the orchestral literature, I knew only three very well; as I checked the music, miracle of miracles, I saw that it was those three that were there. Perhaps I should have confessed that I knew those pieces well and that it would not really be sight-reading for me. But I kept my mouth shut. I ignored my conscience and ripped through each piece with vigor. I paused an appropriate amount of time before each one as if I were carefully studying the complex score, which I was about to read for the first time. I had to work hard at keeping my eyes focused on the part of the page where the notes were supposed to be. A fourth and last piece, which was new to me, was not as hard as I had thought, and I was able to finish with a flourish.

Walking off the stage, I found myself no longer drowning in fear. Then it was announced that only one older cellist and I had made it to the final round. I had grown to like and admire this gentleman during our ordeal. It hit me that we were like two gladiators who had become friends just before they are forced into the arena to battle to the end. Now I had to compete, and that was not a concept I liked. I had been focusing all day on surviving, and that had worked out just fine. What was I to do now? How was I to prepare myself for the final combat when my heart was not in it? Pray to win? That seems a little like a gladiator, who pleads with Zeus, "Please let me lop off my friend's head and cut out his heart, so I can walk out of here with my head up high or at least still on my neck." As my new friend/adversary walked onto the stage for the last round, I prayed for him. It was a selfish act on my part since it was the only way I could calm my nerves.

That friendly gladiator played beautifully, but he didn't win.

Did I win that day because I was the best? Maybe I had little to do with it. Maybe it was because Szell told me to practice scales, or maybe because Ormandy told me I wasn't holding a note long enough, or because those two brave Austrians saved Mrs. Goldberg's life, or because Mrs. Goldberg delighted in yelling up at me on the ladder, or because my mother shamed me into taking the audition, or because Ling had recommended that I play the dazzling, impressive Saint Saëns *Cello Concerto* instead of the subdued Haydn *D Major,* or maybe because Saint Saëns sat down one day and wrote the brilliant music that I loved. Hmm. Sounds like eight people helped me get that job.

After giving credit to all those who helped me get my first symphony job, I was led to reflect on four things, other than people, that I felt were responsible for starting my joyful career. They can be summed up in four words. I sincerely believe that anyone, and I mean anyone, taking them to heart can do as well as I did. The words are vision, motive, persistence, and love.

First, you have to have a vision of what you'd like to do. For me it was to play in the Boston Symphony. Where visions come from would take another book.

Second, I think your motive must be a good one. I wanted to share all that great music with the world. Maybe I passed the good-motive test.

Third, you have to persist at whatever you are working on. Ha, did I persist! I never stopped practicing that cello even when I drove everyone around me crazy.

Fourth, I'm convinced that it's going to be a lot more fun for you if you love what you are aspiring to accomplish and all those around you who are on the same path.

There are two non-fiction books that touched me, and my family, that illustrate what I am talking about. The first is *For Those I Loved* by Martin Gray. (I gave copies to my kids when they were about sixteen years old, and we still have them in our libraries.) The other is Malcolm Gladwell's bestseller, *Outliers,* which members of my family recently gave to each other. I think both books can inspire young and old. Unfortunately they support my son's argument with me whenever I get up on my soapbox and start teaching my empowerment theory. "Dad," Mike protests, "just telling a kid that he or she can do it is not enough. You better warn them that they will have to work their tails off."

For those who recognize that there is something greater than one's self—some call this "greaterness" the grace of God—the opportunity of expressing this "greaterness" is maximized through inspiring musical performances.

CHAPTER

5

A WOMAN'S TOUCH

My first day on the job was one of the most exciting days of my life. Sitting proudly in Boston's venerable Symphony Hall, I was surrounded by great musicians whom I had been watching from the audience for years. That first morning we were to record Bernstein's *West Side Story* with Arthur Fiedler conducting. Right at the top of the hour, he quickly walked to the podium and tapped his music stand for us to begin. From the first moment that the sound of that great orchestra filled the air above me, I knew that all was right with the world and that I was where I was supposed to be. Well, maybe not always way in back on the last stand of cellos next to the bass drum—perhaps a little closer to the conductor— but time would fix that.

The cellos started "singing," and I just grabbed their coattails and hung on for the ride. I had never played *West Side Story* before, but my colleagues had ad nauseam, and the way they looked and acted didn't seem to match the glorious sound that RCA was recording. When Fiedler stopped us to make something better, I swore I could hear the orchestra members grumbling.

I couldn't believe that this kind of behavior was going on in my beloved Boston Symphony. Fiedler might have commented that the clarinets and the horns were not playing together at the beginning of the allegro section. Someone would answer him, "If you give us a clear beat it will be just fine." I was later to learn that this kind of repartee was nothing unusual; it had been going on for twenty years between Fiedler and those musicians who had been in the orchestra when he had been just another player in the viola section and not yet a famous conductor. They were trying to tell him, "We knew you when," and he was replying, "So what. You do what I say, nonetheless." The retorts didn't really mean much. In fact, they were a sort of harmless male banter that had been accepted by everyone— everyone, that is, except Winnie Winograd.

Winnie Winograd had entered the BSO a year or two earlier than I, and she was the first woman to be admitted into the string section. One of the best orchestral cellists I have ever had the pleasure to sit with, she brought to what for many decades had been a male-only institution a woman's point of view. She expressed consideration, politeness, decorum, kindness, tenderness, respect for one's leaders, and all those other good qualities that women have been trying to get men to consider for centuries.

Winnie had been just as surprised during her first year as I had been my first morning with the BSO by what looked like a blatant disrespect for Maestro Fiedler. She had made an impassioned plea to her colleagues to give their conductor the respect he was due.

As is always the case, when a woman tells a group of ninety-seven older men that they have been acting like a bunch of little boys for the past twenty years, they ponder her points and mend their ways. At the next rehearsal Arthur Fiedler was given more respect than the Pope, and the noise level was astonishingly low. Whenever Fiedler corrected a player or a group of musicians, no one responded with the usual smart-alecky remarks. The musicians kept quiet and allowed no expressions to cross their faces. Fiedler was surprised by all this consideration, and I was told that he immediately began to worry that his colleagues were angry with him and had decided to give him the silent treatment. He obviously missed the good old days and the exchange of clever insults.

What Fiedler had mistakenly interpreted as coldness from the orchestra became too much for him, and he soon had a mild heart attack. Oh, well, so much for decorum, respect, and politeness. After Fiedler's recovery, it was business as usual, and that's what I was seeing on my first day on the job. No one was ever going to treat Fiedler so respectfully again, taking the chance that he might have another heart attack.

CHAPTER

6

UNFRIENDLY GLADIATORS

I had always dreamed of being a part of the sound that the Boston Symphony string section produced during that first recording session. The cellos created an incredible blend of sweet and rich tones, which were just like that sound I had remembered hearing at my first live concert as a teenager. When I joined in, I felt myself being carried along, and I wanted to do nothing to disturb the mood. What was so remarkable to me at the time was that many of my colleagues were quite advanced in years. Their playing skills seemed untouched by age, perhaps because they had fused together to survive under the might of the legendary Serge Koussevitzky, who had been the BSO conductor for decades. The strength they derived from that bonding more than made up for any effect the years might have attempted to impose on them. Under Münch, Koussevitzky's successor, this glorious sound continued. I truly enjoyed working and learning from such kind and experienced elder gentlemen.

Unfortunately this atmosphere of mutual respect and noncompetitiveness was to be interrupted for a time in my section. I didn't like the change, and I was soon to be severely tested, not for my musical skills, but for my ability to keep my mouth shut. I failed miserably.

By my fourth season in Boston the beloved Charles Münch had resigned, and Erich Leinsdorf became the Symphony's director. It looked like our new maestro wanted some new blood: The older players began to quickly disappear, and young ones took their places. My special status as the youngest cellist in the section was over as even younger cellists poured into the orchestra. Eventually, even one of my own students, Ronald Feldman, who was nineteen, joined us. All these cellists were great players, and most of them soon went on to principal cello positions in other orchestras. But there was an element of competition that emerged in our group, which I hadn't seen before. It's easy to blame this competitiveness on others, but the truth was that I was worse than anyone. I could pretend to be humble, but I was soon to be unmasked.

When I first came to the orchestra, my older colleagues would jokingly say, "Practice at home," if a musician warmed up a little too energetically, as if he or she were trying to impress someone. Now it was normal for some cellists to warm up loudly backstage with their favorite concerto so that everyone could be impressed.

An upcoming audition for a vacant associate principal cello chair exaggerated the backstage soloist phenomenon, and tension grew within the section of twelve cellists.

While sitting on the stage before a rehearsal one morning, a veteran cellist and I were struggling to read a very difficult contemporary symphony that we were soon to perform. The manuscript was almost unreadable, and we complained to each other about how hard it was to decipher. As we spoke, a young newcomer in the section sat down next to us and put up another copy of the illegible music on his stand. He started to breeze through it as if it had been *Twinkle Twinkle Little Star*. My partner and I listened in amazement; we told the rookie how good he sounded and commended him on taking the time before the rehearsal to study the piece, which we obviously had not done. "Oh, I glanced at a score once, but I've never seen this music before. I'm just reading it for the first time myself," he replied. Now I was impressed— actually, intimidated.

Later, as I confided to Winnie about the rookie's great reading ability, she replied without taking her eyes off the music she was practicing, "John, he's probably had the music out for weeks. I was in the library when he returned it." That was it! My testing time was at hand.

At the next opportunity I had to speak to this brilliant young cellist, I managed to slip in this comment: "By the way, I heard that you had that tough modern piece out of the library, but I'm sure you never even looked at it, right?"

I didn't realize it at first, but I was shaming him. My comment made this cellist so angry that it became the opening shot in a war that I was not in a good position to wage. My opponent sat behind me and would hit me very hard on the head with his bow when Leinsdorf turned his attention away from the cellos. After enduring a rehearsal that involved a Brahms symphony and many stinging blows to the head, I lost my patience as well as my good sense. As soon as the rehearsal ended, I wheeled around and attacked him with my bow. Soon he was blocking my thrusts with his bow, and I felt like Errol Flynn in *The Adventures of Robin Hood.* Can you believe it? Here were two musicians dueling with their $10,000 bows on the stage of Symphony Hall.

I tried talking, hoping it might stop the cycle of violence. No good! Talking was out, bumping was in. This new cellist was angry. Day by day it got worse. Whenever he had the opportunity to walk near me without my seeing his approach, he would bang into me and act as if it were an accident. An apology from me for needling him was probably what was needed, but I was too busy protecting myself even to think about it. I started to go down the egotistic pathway to hell.

My opponent had a habit of showing off by loudly playing very difficult music backstage where everyone could hear him. Thinking that two could play this game of intimidation, I would practice for a month to perfect one of his favorite virtuoso pieces. Then I would casually manage to find a chair backstage near enough to him so he could hear me warming up. When I heard a lull in his playing, I would quickly start my warm-up with one of his favorite pieces, usually faster than I remembered him playing it, for maximum effect, hoping to impress him. I also thought my great playing would intimidate him a little and stop him from trying to impress us. No luck, because he just kept moving on to more brilliant pieces, and I was spending my days working on his literature, which he managed to learn faster than I did. My failure in this game was more painful than the blows from his bow.

About a year had passed since my cutting remark, but things were getting worse. The hate and anger I felt from my opposing gladiator were reaching a triple fortissimo. I thought he wanted to impale me with his sharpened cello endpin. By now I was doing a lot of introspective mental work to figure out how I had managed to get myself into such an unpleasant situation. It didn't seem to change things much between us at first, but at least I was beginning to feel better about myself.

Suddenly the sun came out, the rain stopped, and the dark clouds left. He started talking to me. He was downright friendly. I was so relieved that I immediately went to a colleague in the orchestra to share the good news. I told him, "You know, I think this has happened because, a few months ago, I decided not to be competitive any more. In fact, I've changed my whole attitude towards him. I know I've grown as a person. I believe he's responding to all this. Don't you agree?"

My friend nodded his head slowly and took a few moments to consider my theory before responding. "Maybe you're right, John, but I think everything is relative. Maybe all the work you did on yourself helped, but I think there is a more obvious reason for your change of fortune."

I was getting a little irritated at having my well-thought-out theory of personal growth debunked, and I asked my friend, "All right, what do you think did the trick?"

"I'd bet it's because your adversary is preoccupied. The newest rookie that just came into the cello section two weeks ago is turning out to be a bigger pain in the neck to him than you are. He's just protecting his rear. But then maybe it was all that wonderful work you did on yourself. It's funny I hadn't noticed. What did you say you did?"

CHAPTER

7

A GREAT COMPOSER

Midway through my wonderful nine years with
the BSO, I had the rare experience of seeing up
close one of the greatest composers of the
twentieth century. There had been a temporary
thaw in the Cold War, and both the Soviet Union
and the United States looked at this as an
opportunity to show off to each other some of
their treasures. The Soviet Union had some
brilliant composers like Khatchaturian and
Kabalevsky, and the Soviets offered to have them
and fourteen others come to Boston for a special
week to be present when their music was being
performed. There was only one problem. The
greatest Russian composer, Dmitri Shostakovich,
was not allowed to come because he was in
trouble with the Soviet government. He had not
written music the way Stalin had wanted, and so
he was being snubbed by the Communist Party
and everyone else. I guess our government
threatened to cancel the whole project unless
Dmitri was included. The Soviets gave in and let

him come, but they would not allow any of his music to be performed. For one week we performed some wonderful twentieth-century Russian music, but all of us in the BSO wished that we could have played something of Dmitri's while he watched us from the balcony, sitting by himself. None of the other composers would go near him.

After the last performance of that week, our whole orchestra and the Russian composers went upstairs to a special lounge to celebrate the success of the concerts. There seemed to be a fair amount of good will present. Nevertheless, Shostakovich was still all by himself in a corner, and no one paid any attention to the "leper," or so it seemed.

Then something happened that was earthshaking and surprised everyone. George Zazofsky, our assistant concertmaster, got up and made a toast to "one of the greatest composers of our time, Dmitri Shostakovich." The orchestra members all cheered and yelled. The Russian composers stayed quiet and let no smiles cross their faces. Dmitri shyly stood up. He looked so sad and was hunched over as he listened to our praise of him. It was as if he was thinking, "This isn't going to help me back home."

I guess we all hoped that the honor we were bestowing on him at that moment would remind him of how much he had given to the world and how grateful we were for his music—and his courage.

CHAPTER

8

MOVING ON

Things are relative. During those first years with Leinsdorf, it seemed to me that the back half of our cello section had become filled with a lot of young hotshots trying to outdo each other, when in fact, the change from the Münch days was probably more subtle than most audiences could detect. Overall, we were still a great section. Many of these fantastic young players went on so quickly to become heads of cello sections in other orchestras that there should have been a revolving door in the dressing room. Those stars, understandably, were in such a hurry to go to better positions that a love for blending and teamwork, which takes time to develop, was being replaced in the back of the section by brilliance, individuality, and a little less concern for good ensemble playing. I guess we thought that we were leaders stuck in the back of the orchestra.

Our behavior was not always exemplary, and perhaps that started the rumor that the TV crews were told not to film us. It was probably not true, but as I recall, I never once saw myself on TV in all those years when they were filming the orchestra.

Another rumor circulated that one of our respected veteran musicians came up after a concert to speak to one of our "back-stand soloists." He said, "You know, I was watching you guys tonight and thought you were twice the cellists we had under Koussevitzky, but you played twice as badly." True or not, the rumor pointed to the fact that the rest of the orchestra was noticing our flamboyant behavior.

Sometimes it hurt that we didn't seem to quite hit the mark in spite of all the incredible talent we had. Of course, musical performance is very subjective, but I remember attending a Philadelphia Orchestra rehearsal, in Boston's Symphony Hall during one of its tours, that gave me pause. Several of my colleagues and I were struck by the fact that the Philadelphia cello section seemed to play better together that day than ours did, yet we had some of the finest, if not the best, cellists in the country. Why the difference? One colleague, who eventually played in both orchestras, recently told me that the special sound and sensitive ensemble playing of the Philadelphia was the product of their performing in the old Philadelphia Academy of Music. Its dry acoustics made the musicians work extra hard to overcome the Academy's lack of resonance, forcing them to listen to each other intently. They became a great orchestra in the process.

Comparing sections and orchestras like this brings up a fantasy I've always had. If I were Bill Gates, I would hire a big concert hall and invite all the best orchestras in the world to compete in a Super Bowl of orchestras to find out which really is the best. Every orchestra would have to play with two different conductors: one who was their resident music director, and the other, an amateur, and a poor one at that. The winning orchestra would receive a trophy as well as numerous formalwear endorsements.

This country has so many great orchestras and wonderful conductors that it is silly even to think about which one is the best. Our music schools have produced so many brilliant players that the problem is not how to create fine orchestras, but how to encourage our citizens to fill the auditoriums. Maybe we need more dads like mine who will trick their kids into enjoying music. I remember how I did it with my son. Every time Mike took a shower I changed the radio in his room to the classical station. By the time he dried himself and hurried back to his room to put the rock music back on, he had heard about three minutes of some symphonic music. It worked. He loves classical music today.

Sadly it is no longer the thrill it once was for me to teach aspiring orchestra cellists. I honestly felt I was able to help my students win positions thirty years ago, but now, though I see them improve under me most of the time, they are still struggling to find work in any symphony orchestra. More and more fine cellists are fighting over fewer and fewer jobs. Professional sports leagues are considering more expansion teams, but the number of professional orchestras seems to be shrinking. Some orchestras themselves are shrinking. That is why I believe it's more important today for me to try to interest someone in attending our concerts than to make him or her into another professional cellist. We need audiences.

The showing off period in Boston began to wane. The BSO had always been a great orchestra, but now, in the late sixties, it truly felt that way again in the cello section. More new players, who were committed to teamwork and making Boston their home, came through the revolving doors and stayed. One such player was Steve Geber, who eventually helped me make an important career decision.

All through the early years of my symphony career, I had been trying to hide my competitiveness, even from myself. There was no question that I yearned to move to the front of the cello section, far away from the percussion. In those days a cello section usually comprised twelve cellos. (Nowadays it is normally eleven.) By 1967 I had managed to reach the third stand, halfway on my journey, but I began to examine my prospects for reaching the first stand, where the view was the best and the sound was perfect. Our wonderful principal cellist, Jules Eskin, was my age, and unless I pushed him out of a plane while the orchestra was on tour, that seat was taken for a long time to come. The second chair was also a superb place from which to watch the action. It was held by someone who was many years my senior. Perhaps there was still a chance that sometime in the future I might win that seat with a view.

Then Steve arrived.

Steve, coming from a family of cellists, was a well-rounded musician and at least ten years my junior. He was a superb soloist, but also a great team player. On several occasions I sat with him, and it was always a pleasure. He was so outstanding that he later won the principal cello position in the Cleveland Orchestra.

With him around and all my other talented colleagues sitting behind me, it seemed to make sense for me to start rechecking the odds that I would make that second chair. I began to realize that perhaps the BSO was not the cello section that I was destined to lead. In fact, I wondered if I was even supposed to stay in Boston. A call that I had received earlier in the year from the Saint Louis Symphony inviting me to apply for their principal cellist position now began to look very interesting.

As I seriously considered going to another orchestra, I realized a change would not be easy. My wife, Peg, my two girls, Steffy and Sara, and I loved Boston, our Symphony, our friends, our four-bedroom saltbox on our lovely stream with our ducks. But there was something more important driving me now, something that would make all these wonderful things pale in comparison—mad ambition and a healthy ego. So, after getting the OK from Peg, I called that great Midwestern orchestra on the Mississippi and asked them if they would meet me in St. Louis.

CHAPTER

9

MEET ME IN ST. LOUIS

It was the best seat in the house. The view was better than the one I had had in Boston, the sound was magnificent, and I was finally a respectable distance from the percussion. No offense intended, but I could appreciate them better from up there. As I sat on the stage in St. Louis's beautiful Powell Hall, a tastefully refurbished 1930s-era movie theater, I wished that every other music lover could share in the moment. Being in front was the way to hear the orchestra, and they were paying me to do it. The first cello chair is usually placed right under the nose of the conductor, either center stage or immediately to the right of his baton next to the audience. The Saint Louis Symphony does it both ways.

It had been hard to leave Boston, however, because no orchestra or town treats its musicians better. Knowing that I was reluctant to go, the BSO gave me a year's leave of absence and a date by which I was to make a decision whether or not I wanted to return. This gave me the luxury of some time on the job before I would finally have to make up my mind.

Something that was making me think twice about the move was the fact that, in 1968, the BSO was a "big four" orchestra and the SLSO wasn't. Four orchestras, Boston, Philadelphia, New York, and Chicago, had the very highest level of financial stability and musical prestige of all the orchestras in the country. Was I leaving a sure bet?

Though the Saint Louis Symphony, founded in 1880, was the second oldest orchestra in the nation, it did not yet have the high standing that the BSO did. (The New York Philharmonic Orchestra is the oldest symphony orchestra in the United States.) I was, therefore, pleasantly surprised to find that the Saint Louis Symphony was a terrific orchestra. Within a few years its reputation would soar nationally, first under Walter Susskind and George Semkov, then under our great American conductor Leonard Slatkin, who, I believe, was most responsible for building the Symphony into what it is today. *Time* (June 6, 1982) recognized this by rating the Saint Louis Symphony second in the nation after the Chicago Symphony Orchestra. Though it may not have been the definitive source in matters pertaining to music, it was nice when *Time* jumped on our bandwagon. As I sat playing on the stage during my first year in St. Louis in 1968, I could already see that all I was facing was the opportunity to go from one great orchestra to another. The leap was beginning to look easier and easier. So I let the date by which I had to notify the Boston Symphony pass.   I never consciously regretted making the decision to stay in St. Louis and make it my new home, but I must admit that I had a strange nightmare for several years: I was trying to get back on the Boston stage, but someone was holding the stage doors shut. From behind those doors I could hear all my former Boston Symphony colleagues singing, "Too late, too late, you've missed that important date."

CHAPTER

10

THEY HAVE A CONTROL PROBLEM

During those first years of my career as principal cellist in the Saint Louis Symphony, I found myself experiencing things that I had never noticed before when I was a section player. Of course, much of my attention had to be focused on learning how to do my job well. There was still time to realize that my principal seat also brought a new perspective about everything that was around me. From up front I could now hear all the different individual sections of the orchestra more easily and thus could personally follow them better during their big solos. In turn, I could often feel my section keying on me as well as the conductor as we negotiated our way through the complexities of a symphonic performance. And of course, that indispensable conductor. I began to see him differently too.

My colleagues and I always kept our eyes on the maestro. One can't survive for long without glancing in his direction more than occasionally.

But now, because I was up so close to him in my new seat, I had many more opportunities to interact with him, to study him, and to begin to see more clearly what the maestro was made of and how that set him apart from the rest of us. Besides having genius and talent, a few maestros were quite self-possessed. Or maybe some were a little crazy. A maestro has to be both self-possessed and crazy to stand up in front of one hundred musicians, who were not born yesterday, and expect them to hang on his every word.

The Saint Louis Symphony is a very kind and supportive orchestra, but the musicians, like our counterparts in other cities, enjoyed sizing up anyone who dared to step on that podium and tell us how it was supposed to go. It was only natural that we would have opinions of our own, though we rarely expressed them to our leaders. I'm sure, however, that anyone standing on the podium could have sensed our true feelings. I could imagine how hard it must have been for some conductors to be up in front of a bunch of judgmental know-it-alls like us. Even a self-possessed maestro can sometimes feel as if he has a tiger by the tail.

In the tiger department, guest conductors have it a little easier because they can program their strongest repertoire, impress the audience and us, and then leave town before anyone really knows what hit them. Guest conductors can't get too mauled in the short time they have to spend in the cage with us. We don't always have enough time to find their weaknesses.

It is being a resident conductor/music director that is really difficult, because you have to hang around for twelve to twenty weeks a year, and sometimes over a twelve- to twenty-year period. Thus everyone, including the stage manager, has time to examine each conductor's every blemish. No one can survive that long with just smoke and mirrors, and here is where it gets interesting. How do conductors do it? How did they control and keep us in line for so long?

It certainly helped matters when conductors were good musicians, but something else was going on here, which was almost as important as their musical skills. They used something I call "control-magic." Sometimes we players didn't even know what was happening to us when they cast their spells, but now that I was so close to the podium, I thought I could finally understand what they had been doing to us all those years.

An incident I remembered from years before when I was in the BSO now made sense. That was the time when I must have witnessed magic so strong that I saw it take a grown man and, for no apparent reason, make him leap out of his seat in front of fifteen thousand people.

The leaping-musician incident occurred one lovely moonlit evening while I was still with my former orchestra, the Boston Symphony. We were performing at Tanglewood, the Symphony's summer home in western Massachusetts, under the direction of Eugene Ormandy, whose "control-magic" came from his "voodoo" eyes. No matter where he looked in the orchestra, everyone thought he was looking at him or her. Those eyes, of course, made everyone nervous, but they also made everyone behave and give one hundred percent, one of the reasons why his Philadelphia Orchestra sounded so great. With those eyes, he controlled everyone.

That night, my stand-partner and I were sitting in the last stand of the cellos, right in front of the first bass stand. During that entire evening's performance of Mahler's *First Symphony,* I could plainly see Ormandy looking directly at me. I gave my all, and by the final chords, I was drenched with perspiration. The huge audience rose to its feet to give us a standing ovation. After acknowledging the applause, Ormandy turned to the orchestra to thank us for our work. Looking at me as if to recognize my great contribution to this performance, he slowly raised his arm and, pointing his finger, singled me out for all to see. Now, I knew I had just played the heck out of the Mahler, but I became a little nervous as he began walking towards me through the cello section, his eyes fixed on mine. He was soon just a few feet away from me. With a broad smile on his face, he extended his right hand to congratulate me in front of my colleagues and the fifteen thousand people in the audience.

"Aw shucks," I thought. "I was good, but you didn't have to go to all this trouble." Common sense tried to keep me firmly in my seat, but those "voodoo" eyes were compelling me to rise immediately, put out my sweaty hand to the maestro, and accept the congratulations he was offering to me. Just as my will crumbled in submission to this magician and I flexed my thighs in preparation to leap up and grab the hand that was now literally six inches from my nose, my partner beat me to it. He leaped up and grabbed Ormandy's hand, shaking it vigorously, accepting the gratitude that I knew was surely meant for me. Ormandy, though somewhat taken aback by this cellist unexpectedly popping up in front of him, graciously shook my colleague's hand, and that's when, for the first time, I saw that his eyes weren't on me. His eyes weren't on my stand-partner either. The spell was broken.

His eyes were on the principal bass player directly behind us, who had just performed the famous bass solo in the second movement of the Mahler symphony. When Ormandy was finally able to retrieve his hand, he smiled at my partner for a moment and then turned to continue on his journey. Stepping between my partner and me, Ormandy was finally able to achieve what had been his goal all along, to shake the hand of the principal bassist, who was the true soloist that evening. This latest hand-shaking scene in back of me mercifully shifted the attention of the fifteen thousand people in the audience and my one hundred colleagues to where it belonged—on the first bass stand, not on the last cello stand.

I didn't know how my partner felt at that moment, but I was definitely trying to look as small as possible, hunched over behind my cello while all this congratulating was going on behind me. I don't think I had made it more than an inch off the chair when my partner jumped out of his. But it was such a close call that I wanted to appear as small as possible in case someone saw that inch.

After the concert was over, I wanted to get off the stage as quickly as possible. A little later, as I was counting my blessings and packing up my cello to leave for home, one of my colleagues came up to speak to me.

"I don't know where your partner got that crazy idea that Ormandy was watching him during the concert because I know the maestro was looking at me the entire evening."

I call that "control-magic."

CHAPTER

11

DEE DA DEEDLE DA DA

During my third year with the Saint Louis Symphony, I had an opportunity to view, first-hand, a truly remarkable display of control by a conductor over one orchestra musician. The conductor was the venerable ninety-six-year-old solo cellist, Pablo Casals, an idol of mine as long as I could remember. I was the orchestra musician under his control.

In mid-season I had been invited to play first cello with the prestigious Casals Festival Orchestra in Puerto Rico, and the Saint Louis Symphony obligingly allowed me to leave for one week to accept the honor. As I flew into San Juan with my family and my cello, I could hardly contain my excitement. What an opportunity! I was going to work in an outstanding orchestra made up of great musicians from all over the world and, during my time off, walk through Old San Juan or sunbathe on the island's beautiful beaches. Once again, I was getting paid to enjoy myself. The biggest thrill, though, was the fact that the greatest cellist of all time, Pablo Casals, whom I'd never seen in person, was to conduct a piece at one of the concerts. Casals, at the time, was probably the most respected living musician in the world (as Yo Yo Ma is now), and for the first time in my life, I would have the opportunity to play first cello right under his nose.

As often happens, we forget the lessons painfully learned in the past. Forgetting how my desire to impress once "blew up" the BSO, my imagination started down that dangerous egotistic path once more.

"If Casals is impressed with my work as his first cellist, I'll be set." My train of thought moved ever deeper into absurdity. "Casals endorses Sant'Ambrogio" was next. I could see the management back in St. Louis begging me to accept thousands of dollars more if only I'd show up occasionally. Of course, I kept telling myself not to get too carried away with such nutty fantasies. But with an opportunity like I was getting with Casals, it wasn't easy to stay rational.

On the day of the first and only rehearsal of the music Casals was conducting, I arrived early, along with the rest of the musicians, to warm up on Mendelssohn's *Fingal's Cave Overture*, the music the maestro was to conduct. All of a sudden there was a respectful silence and everyone stopped their practicing. A moment later Casals came through the stage door and walked very slowly out to the podium. As he raised his baton to begin, we raised our instruments and looked up into that marvelous face, which we had studied in photos for years.

I had another thing going for me, I thought, in my quest to impress Casals. This overture started with a six-note motif for the cellos alone. There was no way Casals could avoid noticing my extraordinary leadership qualities as his first cellist.

"De-da-deedle-da-da" sang out from our cello section, music to my ears, but unfortunately, not to his. He stopped us, and I wondered why.

"No, no, not good," he reproached us. "You must make the first note longer, Deeeeee-da-deedle-da-da. Play again!"

We stretched that first eighth note, and again, it sounded all right to me, but Casals would have none of it. He scolded us, "It must be more like the ocean, the waves in the ocean, see the water in your minds. Play again—not too loud. No. No. No!"

Those wonderful endorsements I had imagined began to fade. "Too bright. Your sound is too bright and too loud." I quickly turned to my forlorn section and told them to play the passage on a lower string, which would produce a darker sound.

For a moment, I had hope because I thought that I saw his eyes begin to show approval, but not for long.

"No!" he said. "I must see the grass blowing in the wind. No—play again!" I couldn't see the grass or the waves, but I could see my Saint Louis Symphony raise going out the window and my reputation as a first cellist dropping fast.

After a half-hour of this torture, the attention of the rest of the orchestra began to drift. Hearing those six notes over and over again fascinated only Casals. Some players began reading whatever material they could reach from their chairs. Others appeared to be sleeping. A few actually seemed to enjoy our agony and were wagering on how long Casals was going to do this to us. I could see, out of the corner of my eye, poor Sasha Schneider, Casals's assistant and former second violinist in the famous Budapest Quartet. He was squirming in his seat, looking embarrassed, perhaps because it was he who had been responsible for my invitation to that festival.

We had played that six-note motif at least forty times by now, but our trial was not yet over. Casals was making his point: "You don't impress me, Mr. First Cello, whoever you are. Now you are going to learn what music is really about." Casals was in control and kept us on those six notes for, believe it or not, close to one hour. Then he suddenly abandoned the waves and grass routine and played through the entire overture without a pause. Then he slowly left the stage without saying another word, leaving me and my section dumbfounded.

That night, before the concert, I heard through the grapevine that it would not be unusual for Casals to stop right in the middle of the performance if we didn't play those first six notes to his liking. I was hoping that they were pulling my leg, but I didn't laugh. I just kept my fingers crossed. We must have played those six notes to his liking; mercifully he didn't stop us again. Once we were past those infamous first few bars in the overture, we all played our hearts out for that great man. Some of the inspired playing we did that evening was due to the relief we felt at being free at last, but I suspect drilling us so much on those few notes had made us look deeper into the music. Casals had also drilled those six notes into my brain so deeply that I knew I would never forget them. For the rest of the week, when walking through the old city or swimming in the ocean, I could not escape "Dee-da-deedle-da-da."

After the last concert of the festival and just before I was to return to St. Louis, I had a private audience with the maestro and one of his favorite cello students, Bonnie Hampton. He was very warm and kind and never mentioned "Dee-da-deedle-da-da" or my playing of it. This great artist, one of the most important humanitarians of the twentieth century, passed away one year later. I'm sure that the first thing St. Peter said to him as he entered those heavenly gates was, "Pablo, it was great the way you taught that young cellist to stop trying to impress people and to think more about the music."

Dee-da-deedle-da-da.

CHAPTER

12

STAND-UP COMEDIAN

The longer I played in my new first chair position
in the Saint Louis Symphony Orchestra the more
I could see that the music and the musicians
were not the only things that the conductor,
standing high up there on his podium, was
controlling with his magic. I could see that he
could often create and direct humor too, if he so
chose. Of course, some things, such as
equipment failure, were simply out of anybody's
control, including that of the conductor, but they
had been known to cause a chuckle or two.

An errant cymbal that fell off its stand after a
huge orchestral chord and then would not stop
wandering around the stage in Powell Hall during
the silence in the grand pause before the *serioso*
section of an overture amused everyone, except
our conductor.

The failure, during a concert in central Missouri,
of the percussion section's record player to
produce the necessary prerecorded bird songs in

Respighi's *Pines of Rome* gave the woodwind section the opportunity to jump to their rescue with birdcalls of their own. Even the conductor, Leonard Slatkin, smiled a little at that one.

An exploding cello, caused by an over-enthusiastic musician applying a mite too much pressure on his strings during a wild moment in a Tchaikovsky symphony, provided some humor as well as a lot of excitement as all those around him tried to stay out of the way of the flying debris. But these moments were short-lived and can't compare with the effects that a maestro on the podium can create when he makes up his mind to enter the world of comedy. The conductor Eleazar De Carvalho was one such artist.

The Saint Louis Symphony's former music director from the sixties, the late Eleazar De Carvalho, employed humor as his "control-magic," and he knew exactly what he was doing. The members of his orchestra were under his spell and couldn't wait to see what he would do next to amuse them, but neither he nor the musicians would acknowledge overtly that there was a comedy show going on in their midst. To start with, the maestro had the habit of purposefully mangling the names of every musician in the orchestra: First violinist Takaoki Sugitani became "Professor Saratoga," former principal trumpeter Chandler Goetting was "Professor Chandelier," and former first violinist Wanda Becker had to hear herself addressed as "Professoria Mona Lisa." All of this was administered as if the maestro had never learned the names properly because of his Latin heritage. No way. He knew exactly what he was doing, and he was having fun. He was also controlling the orchestra during rehearsals with humor.

The maestro loved to tease the audiences too. While touring western Missouri with the Symphony, De Carvalho would sometimes wait till the end of the evening's program to have his joke. It was usually the custom on such tours to include a rousing encore if the audience seemed to enjoy our previous efforts. He could pick as exciting music as anyone in this regard. Occasionally, however, he would play something that hardly anyone in a small town in the Ozarks would have had a chance of understanding. Some of his selections would tax the tastes of even the most sophisticated audiences in London or New York.

De Carvalho would come out for his last curtain call after a program of old favorites like Beethoven's *Fifth Symphony* and Tchaikovsky's *Overture to Romeo and Juliet,* which were always a success. He would turn to the appreciative audience and announce the encore: "We will play the first of Webern's *Six Pieces.* Concertmaster, translate!"

The concertmaster, Max Rabinovitz, would stand up, turn to the audience, and announce, "*Stucke Einse.*" The audience would then hear what to them must have seemed like the most horrible scratching imaginable. Webern's twelve-tone, atonal two-minute masterpiece (some might debate this) didn't make much sense when it was played in such a context. After bowing for what had now become only polite applause, the maestro would quickly walk offstage and then just as quickly back again to tell the audience that the orchestra would grace their presence with yet another masterpiece. "Now we play *Zwei Stucke* by same popular composer, Anton Webern. Concertmaster, translate, *bitte!*"

Then Max would get up and announce, "Webern, *Six Pieces, Piece Number Two.*" This nonsense would go on until the puzzled patrons had heard all six, and each piece was announced in both English and German. By the last piece, the applause had diminished considerably, and everyone, including the orchestra, was sure that they were in a loony bin. But De Carvalho had kept the audience members in their seats, almost against their will, and that was what he wanted to accomplish. He wanted to control them.

When our former tuba player, John McNaulty, complained to De Carvalho about the frightening expression on the maestro's face when he gave John the cue for his entrance in the finale of

Berlioz's *Symphonie Fantastique,* De Carvalho came up with a simple solution to the problem. The next evening, when the orchestra again reached the dramatic moment when John, our tuba player, had to enter, De Carvalho covered his entire face with his left hand and turned away from the brass section, almost facing the audience. Then, with his right arm, he poked in the direction of our tuba player, beckoning him to make his entrance. Thus John did not have to see a frightening expression on the maestro's face.

That seemed to get such a good reaction from the orchestra that the next night the maestro did it all over again with one added touch: This time he slightly opened the two middle fingers of his left hand, which was covering his face, and peeked through them at John as he gave the cue for the tuba to enter. John was not amused. Although he could no longer see the terrible expression on De Carvalho's face, whatever it was he saw during his cue, it must have been hard for John to control his diaphragm and steady his lips on his tuba mouthpiece while observing the antics of the clown on the podium.

One incident that our former principal horn, Roland Pandolfi, related to me, proved without a doubt that our maestro knew what he was doing all the time and that he would always make every effort to control everything. After a performance of Mahler's *Fifth Symphony,* which has many important solos for the French horn, De Carvalho motioned to Roland to stand up and take a special bow. This seemed to get such a good response from the audience that the maestro decided to milk it a little; he motioned to Roland to join him at the front of the stage for some more applause.

To Roland, this was going a little too far since many other players had important solos also, and he wasn't convinced that he should be getting all that attention. He declined at first to make the trip. But De Carvalho, sensing the drama here, would not give up. After enduring an embarrassing scene in which his boss kept wildly waving and motioning him to come forward to the edge of the stage, Roland relented and slowly walked through the orchestra to stand beside the maestro. As they both walked off the stage, De Carvalho turned to Roland and said, "We do same tomorrow concert. I like part where I beg you come. Wait long! Is good theater."

CHAPTER

13

HE WAS ONLY HUMAN

Back in St. Louis, the more I played, the more I could see that it was the guest conductor who had it easy, relatively speaking. It was the music director, who was hanging around all the time, who had the real challenge. Each post required different skills.

I remember a great guest conductor who had finished a very impressive week with us. I looked at the playbill to see where he had previously conducted and discovered that he had once been the music director of an orchestra in which a very good friend of mine was the principal cellist. I excitedly called my friend. "Hey, why didn't you tell me about Mr. X before? He's terrific."

"Oh, yeah, we call him Super Sub," my friend answered. "Over the years he lost his effectiveness with us, but he sure can blow away any orchestra for a week or two." Every great conductor can usually be a great guest conductor, but not necessarily a great resident music director.

I've been lucky. Having served under so many music directors during my career, I have enjoyed almost every one, and I have usually even liked them. I'm reminded here of that terrible joke that all musicians know. Question: If you find yourself in an elevator with a conductor and a rattlesnake, and you only have two bullets, which one do you shoot first? Answer: You shoot the conductor twice, because you can never be too sure you got him the first time! Today, orchestra musicians try not to think this way because conductors have definitely become more human. As a matter of fact, if all a conductor has going for him is brilliance and talent, but doesn't know how to keep his orchestra under perfect control, then showing his human side can sometimes get him through. Walter Susskind, my first music director in St. Louis and the man who began the process that built the Saint Louis Symphony into the great orchestra it is today, is a case in point.

Susskind had a warm and relaxed style in his rehearsals and talked to us almost as if we were his children. He was a deep musician, and what he had to say was invaluable, but like a helpful parent, he would often walk around the orchestra making sure that the players had written into their parts what he had just said. This well-intentioned assistance would open the door for his "children" to act up. As he journeyed to the far reaches of the cello section, actually marking parts on occasion, the first trumpet would visit the harpist, the second bassoon would visit the concertmaster, and so on. Soon it was like recess on the playground at the local elementary school. Strangely none of this commotion ever seemed to bother the maestro. As he walked back to the podium, he had the look on his face of a proud father who was thinking, "Children will be children," and didn't seem to mind that things were getting a little out of hand.

In spite of this free-reins approach, Walter Susskind was liked and respected. There was no question that the orchestra constantly improved under his direction. His lack of interest in controlling everybody and everything, different from most other conductors, did him in only occasionally, and it didn't seem to bother him very much, except once—maybe. On that occasion, I remember that he lost control of a piece of his apparel that I know was quite dear to him.

During a concert in central Missouri, Susskind began to really throw himself into Tchaikovsky's *Romeo and Juliet*, which was the last piece on the program. Midway through the music, he accidentally stuck his baton into his toupee, lifting it above his head for just a moment and dislodging it from its rightful place. I was, at this time, seated directly in front of him; thus it was extremely hard to ignore what was happening. Actually, I was fascinated by how many different places a hairpiece could occupy on one's head. First over one ear, then on the forehead, then the other ear, as the maestro desperately tried to adjust the wayward wig. Without a mirror, this was next to impossible. With the addition of conducting a one hundred-piece orchestra during the furious finale of *Romeo and Juliet* in front of two thousand people, it was hopeless. Horror-struck, we tried to keep one eye on the music and the other on the event that was taking place on the podium. Some of the woodwinds raised their stands very high so that they couldn't see him and be distracted by his efforts to control the roaming rug. Of course the scene was beginning to be hilarious, but no one consciously wished the maestro ill. Probably all the orchestra members were praying their hearts out for him, with possibly two exceptions.

Out of the corner of my eye, I could see that the concertmaster and his associate were doubled over with laughter. They were out of his line of sight and could afford the luxury of this insensitive behavior. The rest of us had to keep from even smiling. All of a sudden I remembered that after the concert I had to drive back to St. Louis in a private car with those two laughing louts, the manager of the orchestra, and—who else—Walter Susskind. This car trip could turn out to be even more awkward than the scene I was presently witnessing.

We finished the concert in one piece, and happily the hairpiece left the stage with the maestro. I went backstage, where everyone was laughing, packed up my cello, and rushed out of the hall to catch my ride back to St. Louis with my colleagues. When the five of us met at the car for the trip back home, we were all pretty quiet. The maestro was calm and unruffled. It was obvious that he had found the mirror in his dressing room. I relaxed. It looked like things would be all right, and we would, if we knew what was good for us, forget what had just occurred onstage.

As best as I can remember, after we had settled ourselves comfortably in the car, our associate concertmaster, Ronnie Patterson, unable to resist temptation, commented for all to hear, "Wow, that was a hair-raising performance!"

CHAPTER

14

ALWAYS ON THE OUTSIDE

As the years went by and I settled in as the first cellist in the Saint Louis Symphony, I had a great sense of gratitude for being a part of the exciting and magical world of a symphony orchestra. It was again, as it had been in the Boston Symphony, an honor to be in the middle of one hundred talented musicians, performing great masterpieces under brilliant conductors. The fact that I was finally a first cellist of a major orchestra marked a rite of passage for me. I felt privileged, as if finally I was "on the inside." For a long time, however, it had seemed like I would never get there.

For much of my youth, I felt as if I was on the outside looking in. When I was a boy, before I ever thought of music as anything more than a pleasant background for my day-to-day living, the world I wanted to get into was the world of sports. All the other kids in the neighborhood were, in my eyes, exceptionally gifted athletes. I didn't think I was. Many of the other kids made our high-school varsity teams, but I was lucky to play even a little intramural sport. Being a scrawny only child with musicians for parents didn't help me feel comfortable in the rough-and-tumble sports world that existed on the playgrounds around my home in Bloomfield, New Jersey.

I was too stubborn, however, to let this stop me from trying to get into all the rough pickup games that were going on in my neighborhood. There was no sport I didn't attempt, and each came with some physical cost. Football claimed one front tooth, baseball left my fingers swollen and black-and-blue, and my ankles were perpetually swollen from twisting them in the many dirt holes in our backyard basketball courts. I would moan to myself, "If only I had a brother or father who was into sports, I'd be just as good as all my friends." But that was just wishful thinking to help me deal with the fact that I knew I'd never make it through those sacred doors of my high school's varsity locker rooms. It killed me that all my buddies were inside while I was on the outside.

Several years later, after my high-school graduation, I began to pursue a career in music. Once again I had that same old "I'm on the outside" feeling.

In 1950 there were only four symphony orchestras in the country that paid what we would today call a living wage. The orchestra business was not a financially secure field. Because of this my parents decided that it was too risky to put all my eggs in the symphony orchestra basket; thus they encouraged me to study at Lebanon Valley College to become a public-school music teacher. They felt that this would provide something for me to fall back on if I didn't make it in the symphony world.

In 1951 Lebanon Valley College, a small liberal-arts college in Annville, Pennsylvania, had offered me a full, four-year tuition scholarship to earn a music education degree. I looked forward to attending college, and I will always be grateful for the financial aid and well-rounded education that Lebanon Valley College gave me. But the scholarship also meant that there would be no music conservatory, the traditional training ground for an aspiring orchestra musician like me, in my future. In truth, because I had only started studying the cello a little more than three years before graduating from high school, I'm not sure that I would have been admitted to a good conservatory if I had applied. Nonetheless, my lack of conservatory training haunted me. I thought, "How do I get into a great orchestra if I'm training to be a school teacher?" There I was "on the outside" again, watching my future competition work and train together at prestigious conservatories like the Julliard School of Music, while I was on a different path, taking college courses in United States history and vocal methods for grade-school music teachers—not the best preparation for music students hoping to walk through symphony orchestra doors.

Lebanon Valley College, in the heart of the Pennsylvania Dutch country, was several hours from Philadelphia, the nearest city with an outstanding cello teacher. My father convinced me that, if I wanted to keep any hopes alive of ever auditioning for a major orchestra, I would need to make frequent trips to Philadelphia during the school year to study my instrument privately with a master teacher. My only means of transportation for the journey was my thumb, so I started hitchhiking to Philadelphia on the weekends to study with Paul Olefsky, the brilliant, young, new principal cellist of the Philadelphia Orchestra.

Paul was a great help in my quest to stay abreast of those other conservatory cellists. He was a gifted teacher of cello technique. More important, he had exactly what I needed to inspire me. He was flexible enough to change his approach in an instant if he felt that what he was doing wasn't working.

After I had played a little at my first lesson, Paul sternly lectured me that I was not taking my cello studies seriously and had obviously not practiced enough before making the trip to see him. I would have to work harder in the future. I had actually worked very hard to prepare for the lesson. I simply wasn't that good yet. I think that, in the middle of his speech, he thought that he saw a tear in one of my eyes. He hesitated for a moment. Then changing his tone, he said more kindly, "Perhaps I have you all wrong." And then he began to build my confidence, lesson by lesson, from that time forward by praising every little improvement I made. Sometimes there wasn't much. One cello lesson every other week, even with a cello teacher like Paul, wasn't the same as attending a music conservatory, though it was a help. Just to hear Paul play some of the pieces I was studying made each trip worthwhile. I kept hoping that I was not falling too far behind all the other young cellists in the country.

I looked forward to every lesson, but the trip was usually not easy. After a lesson, I would position myself on the side of the highway in the wee hours of the morning waiting endlessly for a ride back to school. There were so few cars at that hour that I would often lie down and rest in the middle of the road, using my cello case as a pillow. When you're young, nothing can happen to you, or so it seems. Besides, it would often be thirty minutes or more before any vehicle would come along; thus I always had a good two or three minutes of approaching headlights before I had to jump up, clear the highway, and put out my thumb. My best and longest rides were with truckers, curious to find out what was in the tall black case standing next to me by the side of the road. After they had picked me up, they were only too happy to let my cello share space in back with their loads of coal or crated oranges.

This effort to keep all my bases covered still didn't relieve me of the feeling that, because I lacked the background of a concentrated musical environment, which a conservatory would have given me, my chances for getting into a great orchestra were slim. Fortunately the U.S. Army would soon come to my rescue.

Before my third year at college, Paul, who was in his mid-twenties, joined the Navy Band to avoid being drafted by the same army that would later help me become a professional musician. Both the Philadelphia Orchestra and I would miss him. Before Paul went to his base in Washington, D.C., however, he arranged for me to audition for the Boston Symphony's 1952 Summer Orchestra School at Tanglewood, a six-week program that brought together some of the best young musicians in the country, many from leading conservatories. To my delight, I was accepted.

The program at the BSO's school that summer was, up to that time, the most exciting musical experience I'd ever had. Leonard Bernstein was the director of our student orchestra, and the chance to work with him for six weeks was an opportunity I've cherished all my life. I also had my first encounter with my future BSO maestro, Charles Münch. At that point in my studies, I didn't have the knowledge to always understand what he was doing when he did some of his fancy beating. I wasn't the only one who was confused. When I asked Leonard Bernstein, who, as the director of the program, was always present at our rehearsals, what Münch was doing at a particular spot in the music, he just looked puzzled and said, "I haven't the slightest idea." I felt like I was in good company.

At the end of the seminar I received the Piatigorsky Prize, an award of $500, which I believe the school gave to the hardest working cello student. Frankly, I was still such a slow learner back then, at the age of nineteen, that what looked like honest hard work to everybody else was just frantic efforts on my part to stay afloat. I was grateful for the award, but I still felt as if I was "on the outside." That summer made me realize how much I was missing by not being around other would-be-professional musicians during the school year. When my newfound friends headed back to their respective conservatories, I returned somewhat dejectedly to my college.

The award from Tanglewood, however, gave me some credibility in the music world, and when I started my third year at college, it provided an entree to audition for Leonard Rose, the premier cello teacher in the United States at the time. During my audition Mr. Rose listened to me politely for a few minutes. After saying, "We have a lot of work to do with you," he agreed to take me on as a student. Thirty years later he would warmly comment to my daughter Sara, who also took lessons from him, that we were the only father-daughter team he had ever taught.

The trip from Annville, Pennsylvania, to study with Mr. Rose in New York was too far to hitchhike with any predictability regarding arrival times. So I persuaded my father to lend me our little camp truck for the trip. I now drove every other week from my college, with my cello as a co-pilot in the front and only seat in the crowded truck cab, to study with Mr. Rose at the Julliard School of Music. The irony was that I was finally realizing my dream of studying at a conservatory—but only for an hour every other week. While passing all those would-be orchestra musicians in the halls before my lessons, it was hard not to imagine how much closer I might be to my goal if I could be one of them and not just a visiting college student from Pennsylvania. I shouldn't have complained because that one hour, twice a month, with Leonard Rose was helping me keep abreast of my competition, as had the time I spent earlier with Paul Olefsky. Mr. Rose's trademark was his gorgeous tone, and it was imperative for me to learn from him how he produced it. One can only hope I did.

As my college graduation approached, I knew I still had a lot more to learn about my instrument before I would be ready for a serious orchestra audition. With this in mind I took a job as a public-school music teacher in Bellport, Long Island, a town close to the home of Leonard Rose. Thus I would be able to continue my studies with him. After my first and only year of public-school teaching, which I enjoyed very much as I always loved being around kids, and that extra year of work with Leonard Rose, from which I benefited greatly, I accepted a fellowship at Ohio University to avoid being drafted into the Army. This army that I was trying so hard to avoid would soon give me the last experience that was necessary to complete my musical training and prepare me for the career I so longed for. The Army would finally help me come in from "the outside."

CHAPTER

15

DESTINY

One may ask how following tanks through the Texas desert, living with rattlesnakes, and getting blown off the ground firing recoilless artillery could have been as valuable to me as a music conservatory education. Believe it or not, none of those experiences hurt me. In surviving them, I acquired a broader perspective on life. Sounds good now, but I wouldn't have listened without laughing, or maybe crying, if anyone had preached this to me while I was going through my ordeals.

After surviving the first six months of combat training, the Army was to give me a year and a half of orchestral music making, which I desperately needed. This, along with providing free travel throughout Europe, made that year and a half one of the best times of my life. The whole experience was the best thing that could have happened to an aspiring principal cellist.

Before I could get to the "heaven" part of my brilliant army career, however, I had to endure the "hell" period, in which I would have one of the biggest struggles of my life just to keep my cello fingers and musician's eardrums intact.

Fortunately, for six years during the Korean War, while attending first, Lebanon Valley College, and then later, Ohio University, I had been granted successive student deferments. The war ended, but the draft didn't, and my student deferments were harder and harder to come by. I had been grateful to avoid the Army for all those years and had never been tempted to let the Army take me without a fight. I saw no advantage in carrying a gun instead of a cello. Halfway through graduate school, though, my feelings changed.

I started to look at the big picture. If I were really grateful for my country, I thought, I should probably share in the inconvenience that many of my friends were experiencing. Maybe it wouldn't be so bad. Since I played the French horn a little bit in high school, perhaps I could get into a band, and that would improve my chances of having a nonviolent Army career. Besides, my grades didn't look like they were going to be sensational that semester. If I left in the middle of the term, I could avoid that embarrassment. So, with an equal dose of youthful idealism and cowardliness, I allowed myself to be drafted into the Army.

The day I hit boot camp at Fort Dix, New Jersey, I began to have second thoughts about my decision to let the Army take me. I could see that the Army was not designed to be a comfortable place for a sensitive cellist like me. It was obvious that, when the Army said it wanted me, it meant that it wanted all of me, ears and fingers included.

At my first target practice with live ammunition, I was shocked to find out how loud a rifle could sound when held next to your cheek. I immediately informed my sergeant that I was a musician in real life and was going to need my sense of hearing after I left the Army. I also asked, "Do you have any old earplugs around I could use?" He wasn't interested in my dilemma. On top of that, when he did speak to me, I couldn't understand what he was saying. Often I asked myself, "Am I in the right army?" Many of the sergeants seemed to be speaking with a heavy Southern accent that a Yankee like me could make neither head nor tail of. Sometimes I'd ask the soldier next to me, "What did the sergeant just say?" Occasionally, I couldn't understand my colleague either, and then I was sure I was in the wrong army.

In 1956 the Army was a true melting pot with men coming from every part of the country, social class, national background, and educational level. I was learning firsthand how differently the

"American" language could sound when spoken by such a diverse group.

Another problem was that, because I had waited so long to join up, I was now much older than almost anyone else in my outfit. My fellow soldiers were eighteen years old, while I was twenty-four, and with my prematurely gray hair, I looked even older. To put it bluntly, I looked and felt out of place. To make matters worse, at the time of my induction, the Army had changed its philosophy regarding basic training. Formerly the purpose of basic training had been to build up the men physically and mentally to endure the challenges that they would ultimately face. After the experience of the Korean War, however, when the U.S. troops suffered terribly from fatigue during the retreat from the Yalu River, basic training seemed to take an about-face.

Now the emphasis appeared to be on breaking down, physically and emotionally, those men who ultimately would not have the will to survive the challenges of war. The new policy seemed to say, "We will try to kill you, and if some of you survive, you will be our soldiers for the next war." At least that's what we were told when we questioned the insanity of some of the training procedures.

Our sergeants would often keep us up until 2:00 A.M. cleaning rifles and then wake us up at 5:00 A.M. for a hike. Almost everyone was getting sick, and many were ending up seriously ill in the infirmary. I just prayed to get through my eight weeks with nothing worse than sunken eyeballs. After all, I'd probably be in an Army band soon, so I just focused on staying alive. The only relief I had from this nightmare was listening to a few minutes of classical music on a small radio in the latrine while brushing my teeth before lights out.

Right in the middle of my basic training, I was called out of the barracks to play an audition, which I had earlier requested in hope of transferring to a band unit. The only thing the clerk who was running the audition could find for me to play on was a cello with three strings, one less than the rest of the world plays on. I don't remember seeing a French horn, the other instrument I could play. On top of that, I was not in the greatest shape to perform on any cello. I had just finished a difficult obstacle course in which I had pulled myself under barbed wire, shuddered as live machine-gun bullets whizzed inches above me and explosives blew up next to me, and crawled on my back through the mud. With fingers almost paralyzed, a non-conformist cello, and ears partially blocked by the bedlam I had just been through, I was about to try to impress a clerk who knew very little about music, but had in his hands the power to put me in a nice air-conditioned band room or send me back to the trenches with all the mud and loud noises that I hated so much.

I tightened the remaining five hairs of the hundred or so that originally came on the bow he had given me. Then, for the first time in two months, I drew a sound out of a cello. It was more of a grunt than a tone. After giving it my best for several minutes, I knew that nothing resembling a true musical sound was ever going to come out of that box. So I did the next best thing to playing an audition—I talked one. I could tell that the clerk was convinced that, even though he wasn't hearing anything other than my voice, he was talking to a great musician. I saw it in his eyes.

When I returned to my barracks, everyone could tell by my smile that I did not expect to be with them much longer. I was certain that I would soon be heading to a place where my sensitive ears and nimble cello fingers would be safe from the Army's maniacal efforts to destroy them. I just knew that it had been my destiny all along.

CHAPTER

16

SURPRISE!

Leaving Fort Dix was like getting out of prison. Finally the torture was over. Our eight-week basic training cycle ended, and we were given two-week leaves, after which we were to go immediately to our next assignments. I enjoyed my leave at our Massachusetts music camp, relaxing and playing my cello, which I had not seen in two months. I fully expected that my grunt days in the Army were over. My new orders read, "Proceed to Fort Hood Texas for advanced training." Looking back it seems a bit naive that I honestly couldn't see what else "advanced training" could mean other than advanced music training.

There was not one mention of the word "military" in my entire orders. My conclusion made sense to me. No one else seemed to think differently. I was just grateful to the good Lord and that nice clerk back at Fort Dix that I had been taken out of the infantry, because I could never have survived any more guns, dirt, and loud noises.

At the end of my leave I flew to my new Army post in Killeen, Texas. On this trip my cello accompanied me. As soon as I arrived in this little town outside of Fort Hood, I searched for a church with air conditioning, where I could store my instrument. My two-hundred-year-old French cello was not accustomed to 110-degree temperatures, which were common in that part of Texas. I also planned to take advantage of every opportunity I had after Army band rehearsals, where I expected to be playing a French horn, to go off the post and practice. There would be no more three-string cellos or cramped fingers for me. My plan was to have my cello close by so that I would be able to practice and stay in shape to audition for orchestras when I finally returned to civilian life two years later.

After finding a church home for my "baby" and a nice pastor who promised to look after it until I returned, I walked over to the bus station to get transportation to the base. While waiting for the bus I looked around.

Things didn't look good. Obviously it had not rained here for several decades. Dust was everywhere, and the store windows were so covered with locusts that I could not see inside. Other military personnel waiting for the bus told horror stories about Fort Hood. "Did you hear about that soldier who was reassigned to come back here and then killed himself in a hotel in

Austin?" And, "Do you know how hot it is in there? It never gets below one hundred during the day!" These comments were making me feel uneasy. At least I knew that I was in a band, so I'd be spending most of my time in an air-conditioned rehearsal room. I really felt sorry for anyone who didn't have my cushy assignment.

On the bus I was struck by the bleakness of the landscape. The parched terrain of the base seemed to be inhabited mainly by dusty, dragging soldiers and giant lizards. The bus stopped frequently, letting off a few soldiers at different sets of barracks. Soon we came to the band building, but the number on my orders didn't match up with this stop. Now I began to get worried. When we came to our final stop, which matched my orders, my heart sank. As I stepped off the bus, I knew I was in trouble. "Advanced Armored Infantry," not "Advanced Army Music," was posted on a big sign in front of my new barracks. My bubble of naiveté, which had me playing music for the soldiers, burst. The Army wasn't going to quit. Obviously it still wanted all of me, and it was going to take another crack at my precious ears and fingers.

CHAPTER

17

THE PIT

Those next three months at that Texas Army post gave me many opportunities to try my old refrain, "I'm a musician and I can't stand loud noises." Unfortunately there were loud noises everywhere. The U.S. Army was tops in the loud noise department. Day after day was filled with exciting opportunities for the Army to threaten every part of me. Accidental shelling by one of our own artillery units and enduring the incredible noise and concussion of a 105mm recoilless rifle (a cannon) explosion from six feet away were just a few of the many incidents that I would have been happy to miss. After nine weeks of maneuvers in the Texas desert, though, I was still alive with all body parts functioning, and the Army was running out of weapons to turn on me. Just as I felt that I was going to make it, and as I neared the end of the "hell" period of my army career, my end was almost near as well. The Army would come as close as it ever would to eliminating my name from the list of living cellists in Texas. This isn't being totally fair to the Army because this mess I got myself into was mostly my own doing. Nevertheless, the Army was responsible for putting me in a situation that was easy for a novice like me to screw up.

We were on a week of maneuvers in some of the most godforsaken country I'd ever seen. This didn't bother me because I had become a jeep driver for my platoon and enjoyed driving all over the desert in my buggy. I imagined that I was a brave soldier in some war movie. Actually, several weeks earlier, I was in a war movie. An officer had asked our company for volunteers to be in a movie, which was to star Rock Hudson, called *Battle Hymn.* I foolishly agreed to be a Korean soldier. They made me jump out the back of a truck just as Rock Hudson's plane strafed me. I was filthy after the scene, and I didn't even get in the credits. Anyway, I might have been a real soldier, but I was soon to find out that I wasn't so brave.

When we arrived at our bivouac area, we were told to pitch our tents before going out on that night's military exercise. It hadn't rained here in ten years, so why put up a tent? I followed orders in a way, though, by finding an outcropping of bushes and rocks on the desert floor. I literally pitched my tent in the bushes. There was a small smooth area in the middle of all these rocks where I could lay out my sleeping bag. This way no one would ever know that I didn't break my cello fingers trying to drive tent pegs into shale, and I could sleep undisturbed by my sergeants in my private nest.

For three nights I enjoyed sleeping under the stars in that Texas sky away from the snoring of the rest of the company. It was my own private paradise. Occasionally, when I woke up in the middle of the night and pulled my sleeping bag over my head because of the desert chill, I heard strange noises, right next to my ears, which sounded like the furious flapping of the wings of a giant locust. But it wasn't until the fourth night that I realized what a unique resting place I had discovered.

After our maneuvers that evening, I parked my jeep and quickly sneaked up to my private "bedroom." As I bent down to remove a stick that lay where I was to unroll my sleeping bag, I suddenly realized that it wasn't a stick. With my hand still on its way to sweep the object away, I found myself staring into the green eyes of a six-foot rattlesnake. His fangs looked formidable from my perspective, which was probably six inches from my gray eyeball to his green eyeball. The sound that his frightening rattle made was like the "furious flapping of the wings of a giant locust." I immediately stopped my hand on its journey to remove the "stick." This left me frozen in a very awkward position, bent over, nose-to-nose, trying to stare down this angry green-eyed serpent who felt that this was his bedroom, not mine. This face-off couldn't last forever, and it was inevitable that one of us would crack. Letting out a bloodcurdling scream that woke the entire regiment, I fell over backwards out of my nest. Shaking, I watched as two eighteen-year-olds, with more courage and a lot more experience with rattlesnakes than I had (they had been raised in rattler country in the South), fearlessly dashed into the viper's nest and killed the monster.

Our sergeant came running out of his tent to see what all the commotion was about, then asked, when he saw my sleeping bag unrolled on the ground, "Who's the idiot who's been sleeping in the rattlesnake's nest?"

"Rattlesnake's nest?"

After the boys killed my "bedmate" and I had double-checked my body for any tiny punctures I hadn't previously noticed, they slit him open, and that's when I saw why I didn't have any snake venom flowing through my veins. They found an undigested rabbit inside. Now I began adding up the miracles that had just come my way. First, after choosing a snake pit for a bedroom, I had, for the past three nights, somehow avoided rolling over on at least one or more large rattlesnakes, which had been sleeping next to me to stay warm. Then, just before I was to meet up face-to-face with a big one, the Lord had provided it with a tasty meal to slow it down. That rattler would never have missed me with his fangs had his tummy been empty. They don't miss from six inches, and they strike when you move. The medics were half an hour away and would not have been much help to anyone who allowed a rattlesnake to chew on his nose.

From then on the entire company of two hundred men slept outside their tents huddled next to each other in a giant circle. One evening, while lying awake counting my blessings, I observed why this circle of GIs was always smaller and tighter in the mornings. Whenever someone woke up and found himself sleeping out on the edge of the perimeter near rattlesnake terrain, he would pick up his sleeping bag. Carrying it above his head, he would then tiptoe around the unconscious bodies to the center and try to find room for himself by slowly squeezing a place between two of his sleeping buddies. It was nice to see that I wasn't the only coward in the U.S Army.

18

SENTENCE COMMUTED

With only two days to go before my advanced infantry training cycle would be completed, I was grateful for two things: My ears could still hear music, and my fingers were almost as good at playing the cello as they were before I was drafted. Except for a sore thumb on my left hand, which was the result of accidentally plunging a bayonet into it while trying to open a C-ration can, all my appendages were intact.

Now I seemed destined to spend the rest of my Army days in the infantry. I was not happy. Until those last few days of my advanced military training, I had never given up hope that the Army would see the error of its ways and put me in a band or something connected with music. With this in mind, every chance I got during those ten weeks in Texas, I would leave the base for an hour or two to practice at that church in town where I had left my cello. I had wanted to keep from getting too rusty on my instrument just in case something opened up. Nothing did. Only a miracle would get me out of hell now. The Army had decided to make me a machine gunner in Korea, and my orders had been cut a week before. It looked like for me, at least, the loud noises were never going to stop, and I was going to have to part with my beautiful cello for a long time to come. The Army did not encourage soldiers to bring their cellos along when they patrolled the 38th parallel. With time running out, I prepared for the worst.

A day before heading overseas, I heard my name spoken over the intercom: "Sava Brogio, get down to the company commander's office immediately."

When I walked into the room, there were some noncommissioned officers there, and they all began to kid me and act like they were the bearers of good tidings. "Hey Brogio. How'd you get this assignment? Who'd you pay? Who'd you know?"

"What are you talking about?" I asked. "My assignment to Korea?"

"You're a lucky guy. Your Korean orders have been canceled, and you've been assigned to the Seventh Army Symphony in Stuttgart, Germany!"

Wow! I'd never even heard of that outfit. I didn't question their announcement though, because it had to be better than Korea.

Seventh Army Symphony, here I come!

CHAPTER

19

HEAVEN

During the long plane trip over the North Atlantic to Europe, my excitement at the prospect of being a part of the Seventh Army Symphony grew by the hour. I was finally going to get to use my hands and ears, which I had worked so hard to protect for the past six months, in the way that they were originally intended. The Seventh Army Symphony was probably the best assignment a musician could get in the service, and I could see that the "heaven" part of my military life was now beginning.

All the time that I had been struggling to get the Army to let me join one of its bands, Keith Bryan, the first flutist of the Seventh Army Symphony, unbeknownst to me, had been following my trail through the Texas desert and had pulled the strings needed to get me transferred to Stuttgart, Germany. The Seventh had just lost a principal cellist, and Keith thought I could be the replacement. A mutual friend of ours had told

Keith nice things about my cello playing, and that impelled him to work at keeping me from going to Korea. As far as I was concerned, Keith also saved my life.

When I finally walked into the Seventh's Stuttgart barracks, I immediately felt at home. After all, I was among friends who had also been singing my old refrain since entering the service: "But sergeant, you don't understand. I'm not a soldier. I'm really a musician."

The Seventh Army Symphony had been started in 1951 by Sam Adler, a chaplain's assistant, who had the incredible vision of using music to bring the GIs and the German people together during the early days of the U.S. occupation. An orchestra and chorus of American soldiers and German civilians performed Beethoven's *9th Symphony* under Adler's direction, and the concert's great success launched the Seventh Army Symphony. Many of us in the Seventh Army Symphony, after returning to civilian life, entered the great American orchestras like Philadelphia, Cleveland, New York, and Boston. In the Saint Louis Symphony, for example, at one time we had five former Seventh Army Symphony members in our ranks.

The Seventh was actually one of the greatest propaganda weapons the occupying forces employed to win the battle for the hearts and minds of the German people after the Second

World War. Every time some of the real American soldiers, who served as occupying troops, would act in a way that embarrassed the United States Government, the Seventh Army Command would call on us for help. They would send us, clothed in our blue dress uniforms, into the local concert hall to perform Bach, Beethoven, or Brahms for the offended townspeople. The German audiences loved us and reasoned that, if American soldiers could play their great German composers that well, American soldiers couldn't be all bad. And they were right. We weren't all good either. Keep in mind that we knew the Army needed us.

Thus you should understand that it was only natural for us to try to get revenge for all the Army had done to us musicians before we were safely in the Symphony. What we did back then might seem awfully silly to readers today, but it was our way of keeping our sanity while being housed in the midst of one of the largest war machines in history. Our shenanigans were legendary and often made the doctors in those M.A.S.H. units of TV fame look like choirboys in comparison. That probably was one of the reasons the generals, years later, would terminate the group. Also, after the term "occupying forces" was dropped when describing the presence of our troops in Germany, it was decided by the military commanders that the Army no longer needed a great symphony orchestra for its public relations.

I think that it was incidents like the following that actually prompted the generals to eliminate those crazy soldier-musicians.

CHAPTER

20

THE BEARS

It seems that in early 1955, a year before I had arrived at Patch Barracks in Stuttgart, Germany, one of the soldiers in the Seventh Army Symphony took a liking to a stuffed bear on wheels, which he found in one of those charming German toy stores. Before any child could fall in love with it, he bought it and brought it back to the barracks, where the rest of the Symphony could admire it. This triggered, unfortunately, a phenomenon in the Symphony known as "I-can-buy-a-bigger-bear-than-you," and soon the barracks began to resemble the Stuttgart Zoo.

These bears were given names like Onward and Forward. Soon Upward and many others with names long forgotten joined the ranks. These creatures accompanied the musicians everywhere. Soldiers from the Symphony delighted in walking, unshaven, past the guard posts at the entrance to our base, pulling those stuffed animals dressed in little pants and coats. They just wanted to see if they could get a rise out of the MPs on duty. These guards were understandably furious because they suspected that the musicians were mocking them. There was, however, nothing they could do because there were no Army regulations prohibiting soldiers from dragging around stuffed bears dressed in cute outfits.

While the Seventh Army Symphony was going through its "bear" phase, the Army's central command ordered the Symphony to play a special concert in Belfast, Ireland. The musicians showed up at the Stuttgart airport carrying their instruments and their bears. The pilots thought that the musicians were either crazy or just fooling around. The pilots would not let the bears on the plane. This didn't please the musicians, so they refused to fly without the bears. Because the musicians knew how important this upcoming concert was to the brass, they were only too happy to sit and wait until this fact sunk in up at headquarters. Apparently after an hour or two it did. Then that memorable order, which would make a fitting title for any book that might be written about our outlandish outfit, came down from the very top command. It read, "Let the bears fly!"

These annoying artists in uniform had won their little battle with the generals that day. They also knew when not to push their luck. It was standard procedure in those days for every passenger to wear a parachute when flying in military cargo planes that had been temporarily converted to transporting soldiers. The musicians, showing great sensitivity, didn't insist that their bears have their own chutes. They held the bears on their laps instead.

Sometimes these musician-soldiers would display nutty behavior before they arrived at our base in Stuttgart. Another incident illustrates just how much some soldiers wanted to be assigned to the Seventh and to what lengths some would go to enter our sacred barracks. A fine musician in a combat unit in another part of Germany wanted desperately to get into the Seventh Army Symphony, but had no luck because he was deemed essential to his own outfit. Inspired by the Symphony's growing menagerie, he cleverly bought a bear on wheels for himself and pulled it around all day with a short rope. Of course, his superiors immediately sent him to his unit's psychiatrist. The doctor, after carefully examining him and reviewing his case, warned the soldier that he shouldn't fool himself into thinking that he was going to get out of the Army by pulling a bear around all day. The Army was too smart to fall for a trick like that. Then the doctor said, "I'm sorry soldier, the best I can do for you is a transfer. Have you any place in mind?"

CHAPTER

21

MATADORS

Having just come from Fort Hood, Texas, where the "military mind" governed my every step, I found some of the stories that I was hearing about the exploits of members of the Seventh to be less than believable. "They must be kidding," I thought. They weren't, and they were teaching me, by example, how to get into "the swing of things" in my new assignment: "Of course, John, you're here to play your cello and make music for a good purpose, but that's not all. You must let the Army know who you are and that their view of life is not yours. Your predecessors set a great example for you to follow in this great cause, so now you must go out and show us what you can do for them. Tell the Army what you stand for. Accept the challenge."

Well, if the challenge was to stick my tongue out at the military, I was in a very challenging place to do it. We were housed at the central headquarters of the Seventh Army, and it seemed to me that there were more officers, including one- and two-star generals, than enlisted men walking around the company street.

At first I just observed my fellow musicians as they dueled with their superior officers on our way to the mess hall or rehearsals.

"Soldier, where is the brass on your coat?" a major would inquire.

"Sir, I'm a violinist, just coming from rehearsal. We take off our brass so we don't scratch our violins," my friend/instructor would answer.

After a while, the violinist would simply give the short answer when stopped: "Sir, I'm a violinist." He would then walk away, leaving a puzzled major not sure what that meant, but the confusion planted in the officer's mind usually saved the musician. My buddies were great bullfighters. With each officer they confronted, my colleagues seemed to enjoy seeing how close they could get to the horns and still be around the next day. Back at the barracks they became pilots returning from a dogfight with the enemy. "Wow, I don't believe it! I didn't salute a colonel, and he really chewed me out. But when I told him I was from the Seventh Army Symphony, he just walked away shaking his head."

"Don't you guys think you might be going a little too far?" I would question. Sometimes they did, and they would lose the first round. But they always won the second. Standing in front of the company commander and listening to the charges being brought down on them for disrespect to an officer, they would calmly interrupt his tirade and request, "Sir, if you don't mind, I would like to be transferred back to my unit in New Jersey," or whatever. This would stop the angry major in his tracks. All of us were on loan from other units and could immediately go back if we so desired. We didn't want to, of course, but the major didn't know that we were just bluffing.

The major soon realized that if he didn't stop annoying this enlisted man over a petty infraction of the military code, such as failing to salute a superior officer, there was a chance that this soldier might pack up his flute and go home. The major would then have to explain to a four-star general why the Seventh Army Symphony couldn't play a concert the next night in Bratwurst, where some GIs had had too much to drink and set a brewery on fire.

"Major, why was that special concert I requested in Bratwurst cancelled?"

"General, the Seventh is missing its first flute."

"Why?"

"General, I had to transfer him out because he didn't salute me."

"Really? Well, private, and that's what you'll be if you don't get that flutist onstage in Bratwurst tomorrow in time for the downbeat. I'm going to let you go now because I know you have a lot to get done in the next twenty-four hours."

It worked every time. It never went any further, but if it had, I felt certain that our matadors would have come out safe and sound.

CHAPTER

22

MY COMMAND PERFORMANCE

The Seventh Army Symphony did a lot more than just taunt the rest of the Army. What we were best at, we did often and brilliantly all over Europe. Traveling mostly by bus, we visited many small German towns, which in 1956 had not yet built up their symphony orchestras to their prewar levels. Neither rain nor sleet nor driving off a fifty-foot embankment could deter us from our appointed rounds. The audiences loved us and the U.S. Army for filling the vacuum. We played concerts night after night in big cities and small, at a very high artistic level.

One afternoon the Army bus I was riding in on tour was forced off a small back road in southern Germany. Hurtling down a steep embankment, the bus rolled over twice. When my thirty fellow musicians and I were able to untangle ourselves and our crushed instruments, we were happy to learn that none of us had been seriously injured.

I came through the experience without even a scratch, so it was easy for me to run enthusiastically up to everyone, including those being dragged out of the bus through its broken windows, and suggest that we play that evening's concert anyway.

"We'll show the Army how tough we really are, and besides, think of the press we'll get!" In spite of the fact that my "for God and country" spirit was definitely not infectious, everyone reluctantly agreed to take up my suggestion. That night, with a lot of borrowed instruments, thirty bruised men covered in bandages, including one with a sling, went onstage to show their mettle. By the time the downbeat occurred, however, the numbness that the shock of the accident had initially produced in all my buddies had begun to wear off. My friends were now having second thoughts about the whole thing as extreme pain enveloped their bodies. No one, however, turned back.

In spite of this agony, we still gave our all. Our ouches, oohs, groans, and moans never made it past the footlights. I thought that the whole evening was a tremendous success, and the generals did too. They were ecstatic. They were proud that we didn't let a little thing, like a bus driving off a cliff, stop the music. Understandably, few of my buddies seemed to share the generals' feelings or my annoying enthusiasm.

CHAPTER

23

A CLOSE CALL

My tour of duty with the Seventh Army Symphony was the best time of my life. With my cello by my side, I was seeing the world at the Army's expense. I was at long last having some intense and comprehensive orchestral experience, which I had missed in my schooling, not having gone to a conservatory. I was doing all this playing as a first cellist to boot. I played more solo, symphonic, and chamber music in that year and a half than I had in my whole previous career. We made music in many of the great European concert halls as well as in the ballrooms of charming castles and historic mansions. We met the people of the countries in which we played and were often invited into their homes to spend a few days. We saw Europe, in the mid-fifties, at a unique period of its history.

In 1956 the German people, in the process of rebuilding their nation after their devastating defeat in the Second World War, provided us with the greatest before-and-after scenes imaginable. Although most of the buildings in the major German cities had been reduced to rubble by the end of the war, probably half had been almost completely rebuilt by the time we arrived twelve years later. We were fascinated with how the Germans took a pile of stones, put them all back together again, and made them look like the original sixteenth-century house or castle they had been before a thousand-pound bomb demolished them.

After long hours of studying old pictures, drawings, and, in some cases, ancient architectural plans, the Germans would mark every rock from the rubble and designate exactly where it needed to go. If the original stones had been blown to smithereens, they would replace them with new ones of the same material and shape. They cherished these charming three-hundred- and four-hundred-year-old buildings and weren't going to let anyone or anything, such as a little bomb, take them away. We admired their devotion and industry.

When the Symphony played in Berlin several months after our bus accident, four of us, on a day off from rehearsals and concerts, took the opportunity to roam the streets of both the eastern and western zones of that great city. We were in awe at the ruins all around us. The Tiergarten and most of East Berlin looked as if the battles had ended the day before we arrived, eleven years earlier. Some buildings had holes that were twenty to thirty feet in diameter, where the Russian tanks must have fired point-blank at the last resisters. Hanging over all of East Berlin, like a giant cloud, was a strong odor of charcoal and smoke from the rubble and the burned-out buildings that had not yet been cleared away. This was before the Wall, so we could, at our own risk, take a subway to East Berlin and then venture down its main street to "feel" communism. There were thousands of people walking in the streets, but no one seemed to make a sound. Even at a boxing match set up in a public square, the hundreds of bystanders watched the action in perfect silence. Everyone seemed too frightened to utter even a peep.

The eerie silence and the oppression that we felt did not indicate the real danger to us as American soldiers dressed in civilian clothes. The real danger was the possibility that we could easily be arrested by the Soviets or the East German police for doing next to nothing. Although forewarned, that's just what we did—next to nothing.

We had heard that, for next to nothing, we could buy an entire library of chamber music at an East German government music store, the one quality product, besides bread, still available for purchase in East Berlin. The problem was that doing this little nothing was illegal. Americans were forbidden to purchase items that were being sold at this particular store, which was reserved for East German citizens. So dressing as German civilians and bringing along one of our colleagues who spoke fluent German, we approached the supposedly off-limits Communist store to snare our contraband music. We were very careful to send only our German-speaking colleague in and told him to buy either as much music as we could carry back to West Berlin or as much as our pooled funds could purchase.

We waited outside and watched him, through the store windows, buying away. We nonchalantly glanced down the street every so often, watching out for the *Staten Polizei*. Things were going well as the pile of musical scores that our friend was collecting grew ever higher on the store's counter. Visions of all-night chamber music sessions back at the barracks danced in our heads. Just as our buyer reached the limit of our bankroll, we saw that the clerk was asking him for his ID. Our friend unwisely took out his U.S. Army identification card. That was it. We were in trouble. The clerk took one look at it and went directly to the phone. It was not hard to figure out who he was calling. We banged on the window, motioning to our friend to pick up the incriminating identification card and get the hell out of there.

Our friend picked up his card, ran out of the store, and all of us dashed down the street as fast as we could to get the subway back to the West. Wisely we stopped running just as we neared a corner, and sure enough, walking with AK automatic rifles over their shoulders, two policemen met us coming around a building. I'm not sure running was against the law, but no one else seemed to be doing it, so we walked slowly and casually until their backs were to us. Then we picked up the pace again and almost tumbled down the steps to the subway. We spent a nail-biting five minutes waiting for our train to get started on its journey back to safety, and we sweated heavily until we saw the first stop in West Berlin.

I don't know how much trouble we would have been in if we had been caught. Probably, at worst, we would have spent a month or two in jail and lost our cushy Seventh Army Symphony assignments. Almost getting caught was worth it because we didn't come back empty-handed: We now had a glorious war story to tell the guys back in the barracks.

CHAPTER

24

INGA

There I was in Europe, first cellist in a terrific symphony orchestra, practicing and performing to my heart's content. Surrounded by many excellent musicians, I was receiving as much as I was giving. With charming cities to visit and breathtaking countryside to explore, my life could not have been happier, unless a love interest would have entered the picture.

On my first thirty-day leave in Europe, three of us musician-soldiers planned a trip to Denmark and Sweden. During the train trip through northern Germany and the ferry ride across the North Sea, all we could talk about was, of course, what all young males talk about—girls. After months of orchestral one-night stands, we were finally going to be in one place long enough to do more than just say hello.

By the time we found ourselves drinking coffee at an outdoor cafe in Copenhagen's beautiful Tivoli Gardens, we had run out of things to say about the subject. We just looked. We loved it back in our Patch Barracks in Stuttgart, with all the guys and our tubas and clarinets, but this famous park was something else. We'd truly forgotten what women were like, so we made up for lost time and studied intensely every woman who walked by our table. Each woman was beautiful, and it seemed, after looking at double basses for three months, our appreciation had grown exponentially as time had gone by.

An English-speaking tourist guide who worked behind a counter at an information booth caught my eye. For several days I asked her questions about places I never planned to visit, but my real question—"Will you go out to dinner with me tonight?"—was never asked. I would kick myself because, even though there were plenty of opportunities to squeeze in a quick invitation, I never could figure out how it was done, and I would walk back to my buddies empty-handed.

Then the unexpected happened. While the three of us affection-starved men were slowly sipping something sweet at an outdoor café, two beautiful young sisters from Sweden, sitting at a table next to ours, introduced themselves to us. All I could think was, "Oh, is this the way it's done?" Next, the older sister branded and separated us, and before I knew it, the lovely nineteen-year-old younger sister was leading me off to see the sights of charming Copenhagen.

The city grew more exciting by the minute, and for the next four days and nights, until four in the morning, we never stopped walking and talking as we visited every nook and cranny of Copenhagen. Walking was easy, and a little kissing even easier, but talking was a real challenge because Inga spoke very little English and I spoke no Swedish. No matter, we had a wonderful time using the Swedish-English dictionary. With her limited English vocabulary, and the use of our hands, we talked non-stop about politics, race relations, religion, and every other subject we could think of that couples falling in love discuss. In retrospect, it seems impossible, given the limited tools we had, for us to have communicated in any depth, but my memory says we did. We thought we had fallen madly in love.

Our romance seemed doomed, however, at the end of our four magical days together. She announced that she was leaving Copenhagen the next day to go back to school in Sweden. "Wait," I said, "we are going to Sweden in a few days. Where is your school?" When she told me that it was eleven miles outside of Stockholm, I hugged her ecstatically. Stockholm was where my friends and I had planned to go next. I would visit her there on the weekend.

The last two days in Copenhagen, of course, were not as much fun as the previous four. My heart was so heavy that I didn't even visit the lady in the information booth.

When I boarded the train for Inga's school, I found out too late that one Swedish mile equals eleven American miles. When I got off the train, I realized that this was not going to be a day trip. With no train back to Stockholm until morning, no baggage, and not even a toothbrush, I booked a room for the night in the only local hotel I could find. Then I went to the café, where we were to meet, and waited. When Inga arrived, looking as bright and beautiful as ever, my heart was convinced that she was the girl for me. "You know, I have to stay overnight because . . ." She cut me off, saying she knew. She went on to explain that she had already taken a room for herself in the same hotel, but not to worry, of course, as she would spend the night with me. Uh-oh! This was getting tough.

Now the Swedish were farther along in these matters than the Americans in 1956, at least this American, and I became concerned about what would be considered responsible behavior on my part. While she was freshening up in her room, I was sweating it out in mine. Well, you won't believe it, and my buddies, to whom I later related the events of the evening, didn't either, but Inga and I spent the entire night just talking, hugging, and sleeping a little. I need not have worried, because she knew what she was doing.

When I left Inga the next day, I knew we were soul mates, bound to have six kids, living half the year in Sweden and the other half in the United States. We would grow old together, watching the northern lights glow until we took that Viking boat to the hereafter.

My army friends, who had stayed back in Stockholm, were in hysterics when they saw the incredibly rumpled condition of my clothes after I had spent the night sleeping in them. Those clothes remained in that condition for months out of respect for that special evening.

At first Inga and I wrote frequently and passionately, professing our love and waiting for the first chance to be together again. I was still traveling all over Germany; Inga was still at school in Sweden. We were sure we could overcome the problem of distance because we knew that "this was it." Then, all of a sudden, her letters stopped coming. I kept writing, but nothing came back. Months passed. I was heartbroken.

Gradually the pain eased. I began to think about graduate school and the fact that I still had a year to go in the Army. It was possible for me to get out of the Army three months early if I returned for my education at Ohio University. With mixed emotions, I applied for my early release now that Inga was no longer a part of my life.

The release was granted and I started packing. I knew I needed to move on with my life.

Then a letter came. Inga wrote that she had been deathly ill and unable to communicate or, as she expressed it, ashamed to ask for my sympathy. She was recovering and felt that she was now well enough to see me. The letter I had longed for had finally come—but not in time. All I could think was that if only she had told me this earlier, I would have stayed in Europe forever to be with her. My first three-day pass would have found me at her side. Now we would never see each other again because the Army was pushing me out the door and onto a plane back to the United States. This broke my heart and maybe hers too. I don't know. I would sure love to know how her life turned out.

CHAPTER

25

WINNING ME OVER

After a long flight back to the States, I was mustered out of the service and reentered Ohio University. I began focusing immediately on finishing my education and preparing to audition for orchestras around the country. In the spring of 1958 I was getting to know Peg Steffen, a fellow graduate student who became my first wife. Peg and I were married in September of 1958, one year before I won that "miraculous audition" to enter the BSO, the beginning of my orchestral career. The year and a half I spent playing in the Seventh Army Symphony, however, would never be forgotten. That orchestra, with its daily rehearsals and many concerts, gave me the preparation I needed to fulfill my dream of making symphonic music my life work. I didn't always have that dream.

Anyone who saw me as a five-year-old taking piano lessons from my father would never have suspected that there was a musician lurking in that stubborn little boy. I hated playing the piano and doing all the ear-training exercises that my dad forced on me. I was a terrible student. The only things that my father was able to instill in me were mental blocks that would take years for me to remove. To be fair to him, I don't think it is easy for any father to teach his own child, and it is not surprising that it would take ten years for him to break through my resistance. When he finally did succeed in luring me into the world of music, he had to do an end run to accomplish it. He had to be patient, give up the iron hand, and use a little child psychology. This must have been so hard for him because it was not his normal style. To his credit, he adjusted enough to bring it off.

Both of my parents were fine musicians and excellent teachers of other people's children, but for a long time, their interests were not mine. I hated the whole idea of playing music. My mother, an excellent concert pianist and devoted piano teacher, took on the task of starting me on her instrument after some prodding from my father. After a few weeks she suggested that perhaps she should just wait a while before forcing me to take lessons because I didn't seem to be interested in playing yet. My father wouldn't buy this. He was convinced that he could teach anybody anything, no matter how old or young. He loved to teach. Even though he was a violinist, he could teach piano, viola, music theory, solfège, chess, math, carpentry, and Italian to anybody who wanted to learn. During the Second World War, the few years of his life when he did not earn his living making music, he taught electrical engineers how to design the wiring for cockpits in training aircraft for the Air Force. Amazing, since he had never even graduated from high school.

What could be so difficult about working with a five-year-old boy? A lot! I did not want to learn, and I was his son. His decision to force me to continue my piano studies with him was a declaration of war for me and the beginning of five years of two wills battling each other day in and day out. I'm not sure if it was lack of desire or lack of talent on my part, but one thing is certain: I never learned to play the piano. I can still see my mother's face as she observed our battles. Her countenance told me, without her saying a word, that she was not a party to my father's decision. This horrible five-year drama finally ended with my father slamming down the piano lid and yelling, "Don't you ever touch that instrument again!"

I think he was experimenting with reverse psychology, a new concept back in 1942, but his ten-year-old son didn't fall for it. Only too happy to spend more time outside playing with my friends, I never even got close to that big black box again. The battle was over, and I was the winner, or so I thought. My father must have been extremely frustrated when he couldn't inspire his son, his only child, to care about music, but to his credit, he left me alone for five more years. It's considered essential by most teachers, though I don't agree, that to be proficient on the piano or a stringed instrument, children should start these instruments before they are ten years of age.

Finally, with time running out, my Father employed a new strategy to win me over. I think it occurred to him that maybe I didn't want to compete with my parents, who were already accomplished musicians. So when I was almost fifteen, he brought home something different—a cello. My father then shrewdly told me that he didn't think he could really teach me. He arranged to have me study with a friend of his, Mr. Berce, who was a warm, kind man whose relaxed teaching style was very different from my father's more stern approach. Realizing that I could finally do something better than my parents, I actually started to enjoy practicing.

At first, out of fear that I would be called square, I hid my cello studies from my friends. Eventually the word did slip out, but I was pleasantly surprised when my buddies didn't treat me any worse than they did before I had started the cello. In fact, they seemed to be proud of me when I won the first chair cello position in the New

Jersey All-State High-School Orchestra, though I'm sure that it wasn't as impressive to them as it would have been had I made the All-State Basketball Team, as my best friend did. That would have really been something to be proud of. But I was grateful that what I was doing on the cello wasn't making me look too bad in the eyes of my peers. The music business was starting to look better every day. The real clincher came two years after I had begun my cello lessons.

The parents of one of my mother's piano students had offered her the use of their little farm in the Berkshire Mountains in Massachusetts as a site for a music camp. This was something my mom had wanted to create for several years. My parents planned to look it over, and if they found it suitable, they would begin organizing a summer school immediately. The best part of all this was that they were going to let me be involved in running it. So in the early spring of 1949, when I was turning seventeen, our family packed into our old Plymouth and drove from our home in New Jersey to South Sandisfield, Massachusetts, to check out the Rydberg Farm.

As we made our way through the lovely New England countryside, my excitement grew with each beautiful mile. The prospect of spending my summers in the country delighted me, but there was the possibility of yet another bonus for me in this project. I had learned from overhearing my parents' conversations that if they did decide to run a camp, my father would spend only one day each week with us, because he still worked as a manager at Curtis-Wright, an airplane manufacturer in New Jersey. This meant that he would drive up to see us only on weekends, staying long enough to check things out and teach any violinists who might be enrolled at the camp. He would then turn around and head back to our home in Bloomfield. I liked this very much.

It wasn't that I didn't love my father, but more often than not, I preferred to be on my own. He was incredibly smart, which made me feel dumb; fairly critical, which didn't help my self-esteem; and often morose, which scared the heck out of me because I thought I was the reason for his dark moods. To his credit, he often managed to hold these qualities in check just long enough to get something across to me, usually in music, which he knew was important for me to learn. Today I'm indebted to him for this. As I said before, though, this momentary mood change was not easy for him because it was not his style. Since I was no different from any other teenager, the opportunity to spend a whole summer without him looking over my shoulder and without worrying about what mood he was in was wonderful. I was feeling safer and safer the closer we moved towards that little farm.

Playing music began to have new connotations for me: a chance for freedom, the fragrance of pine trees, new friendships, and who knew what else. When we finally arrived at the Rydberg farm, it was everything my parents and I had hoped for. The little cluster of quaint buildings surrounded by dense New England woods, far removed from any main roads, and set on the top of a hill in the Berkshire Mountains looked like the ideal place to fulfill my mom's vision. My parents quickly agreed to join with the Rydbergs to start what would be known for the next thirty years as Red Fox Music Camp. If you are curious to see what I was so excited about, Google "Red Fox Camp, Sandisfield, Massachusetts, 1950." You will see film footage from our camp's second year. This camp would inspire three or four thousand young people, who still remember fondly what they experienced in the beautiful Berkshire Mountains.

"Camp" was also a concept that I would equate with "home and family" for most of my life. Being an only child always left me longing for a large family. Later, as my own kids grew up and then moved away, I used my camp to fill the void.

On our drive back home to New Jersey that evening, for the first time in my life I was grateful that my parents were musicians. My young imagination ran wild with all the exciting outdoor activities that I would soon be involved in that coming summer. It turned out, however, that one of the first things I would get to do at Red Fox would have nothing to do with music. It would not be too pleasant either, and it would be something that even my wild imagination couldn't conjure up.

CHAPTER

26

DAUNTING TASK

Red Fox Music Camp began that summer in 1949 when my mom took thirteen of her piano students and me, the sole cellist, to the Rydberg farm in South Sandisfield, Massachusetts, to study music. I would spend the next thirty years of my life involved with my mom's creation. In 1979, when we closed the camp, which was now in New Marlboro, Massachusetts, we would have a student enrollment of one hundred seventy students, thirty-five faculty, and, in my opinion, the best softball team in the Berkshires Camp Conference.

Of the three or four thousand students who attended over the years, many went on to win places in major orchestras in the country. Just as important, the rest became music-loving doctors, plumbers, teachers, lawyers, and what have you. While touring with the Saint Louis Symphony, I was constantly seeing former campers at our concerts. They would come up to me and ask, "Do you remember me?" I usually did. At least five campers joined the Boston Symphony Orchestra in a ten-year period, three directly from the camp. Their moms had packed them away to camp for the summer, and they never went home.

My mother built quite a camp. It was unusual, I thought, for such a small, privately-owned music camp to have had such an impact on the musical scene. But my mother was an unusual lady, and she would give a scholarship to anybody who needed one. She provided scholarships out of her own pocket. She knew that to have a great camp, she had to have a lot of talented, dedicated kids around, as well as those who were playing just for the joy of it. The only way many of these young musicians could take part was if she helped them financially. My mother's bottom line was for all campers to enrich their lives with music, regardless of their abilities.

We started small. For a month each summer we moved into a barn, which was the girl's dorm and concert hall; a converted corncrib, which served as the boy's dorm; a small one-story house with two bedrooms and a kitchen; and two outhouses.

One weekend just before the camp was to open that first summer, a pre-camp inspection of the facilities by my father revealed that one of the outhouses was overflowing, and someone had to fix it. This someone turned out to be me and my life-long friend, Joan Napoliello. Joan, a fifteen-year-old piano student of my mother's, was one of the reasons that Red Fox would have such success in the future. She had so much energy that she eventually taught piano and theory, cooked, drove a bus, and lifeguarded during the thirty years that she was a part of our camp. But all that was in the future. On that early spring day in the Berkshires, we were just beginning, and it would not be the first time that we would be asked to get our hands dirty in order to fulfill my mother's vision. We would, before we were finished, get more than our hands dirty, and for what we did we should have received the National Medal of Honor.

My father, after finishing his inspection, was about to leave the camp and drive back to our home in New Jersey. He explained that there were two possible ways of attacking the problem: We could dig a new hole and move the little out-house over to it, and then go back and cover up the "mess," or tip over the little building and carefully dig up the mess. Then, even more carefully, we could haul the mess in a wheelbarrow far out into the woods somewhere and leave it.

Joan and I looked at each other slightly in surprise. We didn't realize that this was part of being involved with a music camp. After the usual griping that normal teenagers do before any assignment, we began studying our options. We weren't crazy about option number two, so we

142

chose option number one—digging a new hole. By the time my father reached our home in New Jersey four hours later, we had hardly made a dent in the rock-infested New England soil. Our hole would hardly have provided relief for the camp's cat. At the rate we were going, we would never get back to practicing our instruments. We looked at each other, and knowing that it would take days of digging before we would have accomplished anything substantial, we contemplated option number two. After all, how bad could it be? Besides, we wanted to get this stupid job over with fast and get back to making music.

At first we made every effort not to get any of the "mess" on us as we shoveled away. We wore gloves, boots, and clothes that we never expected to use again. It began to rain, and the "mess" became messier. Soon we were slipping and sliding around dangerously close to the hole that we were emptying. To make matters worse, the aroma from that putrid pit was beginning to affect our minds, and we began to lose it. We had started out being quite fastidious, but the dreariness of the task made us careless. I'm not sure who threw the first "mess," but it didn't go unanswered. In the beginning there were just a few near misses that we thought were funny. No harm was intended, but one accidental direct hit to the small of my back changed all that. What at first was a playful little exchange turned into a serious all-out war.

We may have been laughing during the battle, but that didn't mean that we weren't in earnest about "destroying" our opponents. It seemed that no part of our anatomies was spared as a torrent of "shells" from our shovels catapulted through the New England air with remarkable accuracy. Soon our clothes were ruined, and it would later take hours in the shower for us to be able to stand ourselves.

After a particularly accurate round of missile exchanges, the humor of what we were doing began to escape us, and we stopped fooling around. During our truce we let the rain clean us off a little. Then we returned to our work, completing the daunting task without any serious losses other than dignity and a sense of smell. Later in the week Joan and I proudly presented my father with one completely empty outhouse for his inspection. Then it was back to practicing our music, which was truly a joy in comparison.

Aside from our bathroom worries that first summer, making music at that little camp in the Berkshires was a glorious experience. It was well worth all the effort that went into getting the place ready for the campers, and it sealed my commitment to making music my lifework. But both Joan and I hoped that things connected with Red Fox weren't always going to be as challenging as that first spring had been. At least we hoped that the Rydbergs might consider adding some more indoor plumbing.

CHAPTER

27

THE RACER

The first Red Fox Music Camp sat at the end of a
long dirt road. From our hilltop site there was
nothing to see but forests and mountains. We
were in the middle of nowhere, and nowhere was
gorgeous. Even my initial responsibility as our
camp's outdoor plumber couldn't dampen my
enthusiasm for our music camp. That first
summer of music and hiking in the beautiful
Berkshires was the beginning of a love affair that
has never ended. I was hooked on music, and the
camp had done it. For many of the next thirty
summers I would often sit under some old apple
tree on top of a hill with a gorgeous view, take my
cello out, put its endpin on a piece of wood, and
practice my music for hours. The occasional
visiting bug never bothered me because chasing it
away gave me a break from my practicing,
allowing me time to enjoy the beautiful
countryside.

As the years went by, our little camp just kept growing and growing. Although during those years I had gone off to college, spent two years in the Army, and joined the BSO in 1959, my body and soul were never far away from those beautiful hills in western Massachusetts.

In fact, eventually I found myself physically in two different places at once.

Once I began the juggling period of my life, I had to play many different roles just to survive. In 1960, as I was helping my mom run Red Fox in New Marlboro, I was also playing in the BSO, which was at its summer home some fifty miles away in Lenox, Massachusetts. Driving one hundred miles a day to meet my commitments as a cellist at Tanglewood as well as a camp director and teacher at Red Fox, I soon became a pretty good racecar driver and quick-change artist. Playing cello with the BSO was the easy part. Taking care of all my responsibilities at Red Fox was more challenging.

Besides teaching, I enjoyed being the resident groundskeeper, barn painter, trash collector and, of course, the camp emergency plumber. I'm now starting to lose my hair because back then, I was putting on so many different hats. At 9:30 A.M., after teaching a student, I would often don my racecar driver's helmet, jump in the car with my cello, and roar down old Route 59, balancing my breakfast on a plate in my lap. I would drive seventy or eighty miles per hour on winding New

England roads to get on the stage in the shed at Tanglewood for my BSO rehearsal before 10:30 A.M. After the rehearsal ended, I would again roar past those beautiful elms, maples, and rough rock walls that lined the narrow roads through the lovely Berkshire Hills back to Red Fox. As soon as I got back to the camp, my wife, Peg, would hand me a sandwich and fill me in on all the interesting things that might have occurred there while I was fiddling away with the BSO.

Occasionally, like the time I had to solve another one of those camp plumbing problems, I would have second thoughts about my dual responsibilities. After spending an afternoon in swampy woods, knee-deep in muck, lifting one hundred pounds of plastic pipe filled with water, and cleaning up messy bathrooms, my love affair with camp began to wane just a little. There was never much time to ponder my dilemma at moments like that because there was usually a concert to play in the evening with the BSO. After a quick change of clothes, I would grab my cello, jump into my car, balancing my supper on a plate in my lap, and continue that endless race, which went on for nine years, back and forth across western Massachusetts.

CHAPTER

28

WHAT'S IN A NAME?

By 1965 our Red Fox Music Camp was a success in just about every way but one. We had plenty of students and teachers. We had some forty buildings with more than enough space in which to practice, rehearse orchestras, and hold music theory classes. By now we had two tennis courts, a baseball diamond, a pool, and a pond. I had personally planted about forty pine trees along our roads, which provided some nice landscaping. Sounds good, but the camp was in real trouble.

Some of our faculty members were winning principal positions in the Philadelphia and Chicago Symphonies. We had started our own faculty chamber music series, which the public and the students loved, and we had outstanding visiting artists who would give freely of themselves to our students. We were able to talk pianist Gary Graffman, cellist Zara Nelsova, violinist and concertmaster of the BSO, Joseph Silverstein, and even my boss, Erich Leinsdorf, who was the BSO conductor, along with many other famous musicians, into working with our campers and accepting nothing in return but our gratitude. We were failing miserably in one area, however.

We had all levels of talent and abilities in the student enrollment, which both my mother and I thought was so important. Many of our top students were entering major orchestras directly from camp. They were learning tons of music, making many new friends, having loads of outdoor fun, and even obeying curfew. Nevertheless, the camp still had one big problem.

Red Fox was turning into a dump. Our students were slobs. They were too busy to clean their rooms. They could care less about the junk that they were strewing all over the beautiful, broad green lawns, which I was so proud of. "I'm sorry, Mr. S, but I had quartet rehearsal at eight this morning! I didn't have time to make my bed or clean up my room." My latest hat was a street-cleaner's cap as I spent more and more time picking up soda cans, cigarette butts, and every other piece of junk that teenagers love to avoid throwing into the trash can. They were simply too busy to bother, and my threats and screams worked only for a day or two. Trying to make one hundred seventy young people be neat without the use of a gun and a whip is impossible. I had just about given up hope when someone came along who could solve my problem. I played him for all it was worth.

One weekend I went to visit another camp in upstate New York. When I returned to Red Fox the next day, everybody ran up to me and told me that the State Health Inspector had visited Red Fox while I had been away. He was going to close the camp if we didn't clean up our act. He promised that he would come back next week and nail the doors shut if we didn't pass his next inspection. Everyone feared that there was a serious possibility that camp could soon be over and that everyone would have to go home early. I feigned shock and fear, but inwardly I knew that I had just hit the jackpot. Looking at all those teenagers, who were thinking that all the fun that they were having might end because of a decision by the State Health Inspector, I realized what I had just found—my savior. The best thing about this savior was that I didn't even have to pay him to clean up my camp; the Commonwealth of Massachusetts did.

First I found out what major infraction he had discovered, so as not to repeat it and run the risk of being shut down. I wanted to scare the heck out of those kids and get them to, literally, clean up their act. But I didn't want to fail for missing some silly technicality.

The inspector was upset with more than a technicality. His general inspection of the grounds didn't reveal too many problems, but he was furious when he saw the inside of one of the large cabins where many of our boys were housed. Our kids slept on those old army surplus beds, which could be put together to form triple and quadruple bunks. The sky was the limit. You could build them on top of each other as high as your ceiling or the supply of beds would allow.

The boys in this cabin had taken advantage of an ample supply. They had built thirteen of them into a free-form, grotesque structure so high that it would be possible for the boy on the top bunk to plunge down two stories to the floor and break his neck if he rolled over too far in his sleep. This hurt us, but the real killer was a pile of dirty clothes, reaching almost to the rafters, which the inspector had found in the corner of that same skyscraper bunk room. This ugly pile of clothes had a shiny object sticking out of the middle of it. When the inspector pulled out the tray with week-old food on it, the condemnation papers were all but drawn up.

Well, we dismantled the tower of beds, put the tray back in the kitchen, did the laundry, and generally began to tidy up around the whole camp. It was a miracle. All I had to do was remind everyone that the inspector was coming, and presto, beds were made, clothes were put away, and bathrooms were cleaned. We barely passed the inspection the next week, but slowly, but surely, things began to improve from that point on, my life became a lot easier. The power of the words "health inspector" was awesome. By the next summer the momentum was building, and this man was becoming a god in the minds of my students. This was great for me, as I could relax a little and even have time to practice the cello occasionally. The mere mention of that man's name struck fear into the hearts of my messy musicians, and even I was surprised at the reaction I got one afternoon when I whispered his name in the concert hall of our beautiful barn.

The basement of that barn, which was on the ground level and had lots of windows, served as a perfect dining hall for two hundred ten people. Its kitchen was always the first stop for the health inspector when he made his periodic visits. One afternoon I just happened to be talking to the cook as the inspector walked in the door. He caught her on her knees scrubbing the floor with a brush and a pail of soapy water, which was a great start for us. He didn't know that a few moments earlier, she had spilled a dessert, and she was simply wiping it up. That floor was very rough concrete, and nobody had given it that much attention in years.

"Aha, I see you are making this floor spotless. Wonderful!" The cook stopped scrubbing and looked at me, and I at her. After being frozen for a few seconds, we started to nod our heads slowly in agreement with his assessment of the situation.

"Yes, just doing our daily cleaning," I responded.

As the "feared one" began poking around our shelves, his back was turned to me, and I motioned as best I could to the cook, who was still on her knees, to stall him as long as she could. My mouth was forming the words "keep him here while I go warn the rest of the camp." Then I turned and quietly slipped out the kitchen door to sound the alarm.

I could hear our student orchestra upstairs reading through a Brahms symphony. I knew that I had to let the orchestra members be the first to hear the news about who was downstairs in the kitchen with the cook and was soon to visit their rooms. All I did was open the barn doors leading to the auditorium and whisper to all those unsuspecting campers onstage, "The health inspector has just arrived." This occurred at a moment when John Covelli, our camp conductor, had stopped the rehearsal to correct a phrasing in the violins. Within a few seconds the entire orchestra completely vacated the stage, and you could see sixty kids running madly across the fields to get to their dorms two hundred yards away, where their laundry might be hanging out the window or the toothpaste cap might be off. It happened so fast that John Covelli was still finishing his instructions to a lot of violins, but no players. His back was to me when I had whispered the important news, so he had not known what had happened. He turned to me and asked, "Was it something I said?"

We passed with flying colors that day, because an army of "cleaners" was always one step ahead of the inspector. The kids threw underwear, bras, and half-eaten apples into the first drawers that they could find. They then rushed to lie on their beds, casually reading books, often upside down, when he entered their rooms.

Our camp was finally shaping up. The next couple of years saw such improvement that we almost changed our name to Clean Fox. The words "health inspector" were music to my ears. They had such a ring to them, and used judiciously, they gave me such a feeling of power.

CHAPTER

29

FINAL HAT

In 1968, driving too fast around a sharp curve on a winding country road outside of Stockbridge, Massachusetts, and almost smashing into two cars that had already collided made me realize just how dangerous what I had been doing for the last nine years had been. Racing across western Massachusetts for six to eight weeks each summer to fulfill my commitments in New Marlboro and Lenox had left me dead tired, but not dead—yet.

I tried to leave our camp earlier each day so that I wouldn't have to race so fast over those treacherous back roads to my rehearsals and concerts with the BSO at Tanglewood outside of Lenox. Alas, my style was and always has been to work up to the last minute and then dash. It drove my wife, Peg, crazy. I never could seem to change the bad habit. Seeing that terrible wreck, with one fatality, made me think seriously about what I was doing. This accident may have been one of the reasons that I left the Boston Symphony and went to the Saint Louis Symphony. I knew that I had to stop tempting fate with all this wild driving, and if I had to spend my summers in the Midwest playing with the Saint Louis Symphony, the temptation would be gone. There was no way that I could commute thirteen hundred miles each day. I would be forced, finally, to take off my racing helmet. I was, however, going to have to put on one more hat before I would be finished.

Once Peg, our children, and I moved permanently to St. Louis and I started playing in the Symphony, I was able to take only a week off each summer to visit the camp. Peg and I, with our three children, would drive to Red Fox each summer. I would spend a week cutting grass, sweeping away cobwebs, painting weathered buildings, and anything else I needed to do to get camp ready for its opening. Then I would leave my family in New England and return alone to the Saint Louis Symphony and the exciting Midwestern tornadoes.

The camp seemed to go on quite well without me. My mother and Peg felt that they needed someone to take my place as assistant director. First Jack Ervin, my pianist roommate from college, then Bill Workinger, another pianist and clarinetist college chum, and finally Willy Haroutonian, who became a violinist in the National Symphony, took turns at being the assistant director of our camp in my place. Each did a great job. All went well, and I was able to help by providing little bits of advice on the phone. But just when it looked like my commuting days were over and I could relax, I got an urgent call from my wife that made me run for my suitcase.

The sixties and seventies were drug-filled years, and our country was having a hard time keeping those drugs from flooding across our unprotected borders. (Not that it's any different today.) It looked like Red Fox, too, might have had a border problem, because the perimeters of our camp, with seventy-eight acres of wooded hills, could also be quite porous. Peg had to be careful about how she spoke that evening, because the only phone at the camp was in the office, and the campers were nearby.

"You remember what we talked about before you left to go back to St. Louis?" she asked.

"Drugs?"

"Yes!"

"Do you need me to come there?"

"Probably."

"OK. I'll take the first plane out of here."

The Symphony understood my problem and gave me a week off to fly back east and try to get to the bottom of it. I made sure I packed my interrogator's hat for the trip.

The moment I arrived in New Marlboro, I made some inquiries: "Is the whole camp tripping out?"

"No, we don't think so, but we have these two government agents who are on our backs, and we need to convince them that the rest of the students are clean, or they won't go away. All this is hurting the morale of the camp," my wife answered.

It seemed that, because the Berkshires were flooded with artists, classical musicians, rock musicians, and dancers in the summer, the entire area was suspect. (The Government, I guess, thought that most artists were hippies.) Someone high up in the drug-fighting world decided that this was probably one of the biggest hotbeds of drug activity on the East Coast. They may have been right. They also had decided to send agents into our hills to root out the stuff.

Red Fox, we later found out, was chosen to be checked out because one of the young drug agents sent into the area had once attended our camp as a brass student. The agency sent him to us in the guise of a sailor on leave, who just wanted to help out his old music camp for a week, because, he claimed, he had nothing better to do with his time. We needed our students to do everything at our camp except teach, so we were happy to have another helping hand and took him up on his offer. We had fallen for his ploy.

Now Red Fox was not a hotbed of drug activity, but there was one incident, which I had been called in for, that rang the alarm bells and got everyone in the camp excited. One student had introduced three other students to an illegal substance, and this agent just happened to be there when our amateur pusher was hawking his wares. But our undercover trombonist did not solve the problem, nor did his superior, who came later, ready to smash open each camper's footlocker. Nor did I solve it. The real detectives at Red Fox that summer were my mother and Nurse Denny. They were the ones who broke the case of "The Crazy Camper Caper."

My mother always read everyone else's mail, diary, or whatever else the kids were foolish enough to leave lying around for prying eyes like hers to devour. This was the way she kept her fingers on the pulse of the camp. She was the research department for our spy agency. Nurse Denny, on the other hand, could mysteriously get the campers to rush up to her at the weirdest hours and confess their innermost secrets. She was the ideal field agent. Conductors could take a lesson from her in "control-magic." (Imagine an orchestra player running up to a conductor and confessing, "Oh, I rushed a little at letter S, and I think I was too loud at 8 before M," after the maestro had simply zapped the orchestra a few times with Nurse Denny's "control-magic." You'd have to have a big book to record all the confessions.)

Nurse Helen Denny was definitely not your run-of-the-mill nurse. A close inspection of her at work in her infirmary might surprise you, because very few people, in a camp of over two hundred students and faculty, ever became or stayed sick. She must have done something right. Helen Denny could usually be found in her crowded trailer infirmary patching someone up. Only Helen knew, in the mess she allowed to build up in her world, where anything was, including the bandages; even she couldn't find them right away. She'd have to search for a while, which was great, because the kid was really there only to talk, and the scraped knee could wait. "Let's go see Nurse Denny" was the most popular refrain in camp.

If Helen wasn't in the trailer, she could be found in one of two other places: walking the fields collecting herbs, which she administered freely and stored on top of the bandages in the refrigerator on top of the salami, or playing bridge up at my house, which was situated on our camp's highest hill. (We had built this house so that we could get out of what was now Helen's trailer infirmary.)

Helen loved bridge almost as much as my wife did, and the two of them were always trying to get up a game. Bridge was all right, but what I really found interesting was trying to follow Helen's famous train of thought. While studying a good bridge hand that she was holding, and with all of us expecting a bid of three of hearts, Helen would say, "John, I think you should do that."

"Do what?" I'd ask, puzzled at where she was coming from.

"Dig that extra ditch by those tents that are getting flooded."

"Helen, it was last week that I talked to you about those ditches. How is anyone supposed to understand you if you are going to talk in such a fragmented way?"

Then we would all laugh.

My mother did understand her, however, and I think that the whole routine of Helen's carrying a sentence over two or three days was actually a code that she'd developed with my mother. If Helen lets drop to my mother on Monday that Suzy, Mary, and Jane had been in the woods with Billy, and then on Tuesday Helen blurts out, "And Billy gave them all a half of an," and finally on Wednesday, "LSD pill," emerges from Helen's lips, Bingo! The code is heard loud and clear by Mrs. S. My mother would rush back to her laboratory to study all the evidence she had compiled during her slow, casual walks through the girls' bedrooms. Then she would take appropriate action.

Now in the case I've just described, the code was actually transmitted over a shorter period of time, but I guarantee that anyone following Helen around that day, as she seemed to talk aloud to herself, would not have known what the dickens she was talking about.(Except my mother.) So why should she feel guilty for divulging confidences, since nobody understood her anyway? (Except my mother.) Helen's trailer infirmary was our counterintelligence headquarters and the envy of the FBI and the CIA. What was so nice about our camp's counterintelligence was that its awesome power was applied gently.

We immediately removed the older student, whom we suspected of carrying the stuff over our borders; then we counseled the three young people, who had been foolish enough to "taste" the poison, and urged them to stay clear and stay on. This turned out to be very important because we immediately earned the trust of just about everyone in the camp. We had turned our innocent students into a huge body of spies, double agents, informants, and just plain squealers that the KGB would be proud of. We were able to convince the kids that if they supplied us with the proper information, no one would be hurt or thrown out, only the drugs would be. For the next six years or so, most everyone worked together to make Red Fox into a real Clean Fox, and even pot that arrived in the mail was often handed over to me as soon as the student realized what it was. A pot party for us was the act of flushing pot down the toilet, and I'm sure that a lot of our septic fields have some interesting plants growing above them.

To appease the second agent and keep him from breaking into the campers' lockers and dresser drawers, I promised him that I would get information from the students that would prove that there were no more drugs at Red Fox. I then brought eight kids who we felt had important information about "The Crazy Camper Caper" up to my house for interviews. We gave them milk and cookies, and then we asked them to read and relax in several different rooms. They couldn't talk to each other and make up a common story. I had read Louis Nizer's *A Day in Court* on the plane to Massachusetts, so I knew that I was ready to question the students in order to obtain the scoop we needed to prove to the panting agent that we were now clean.

In conclusion, I put on my final hat, the one with "Interrogator" written on the front. Then I used all the techniques of "third party" negotiations that I could think of to close "The Crazy Camper Caper" to the satisfaction of the drug agent breathing down my neck. In fact, he stayed in the living room and looked menacing as I visited each of the kids, in our different bedrooms, for a chat. "You know, Billy, that guy in the other room wants to break into our private stuff, but if you can just tell me . . ." Well, you know the routine. Everyone's story checked out; everyone's information was the same. This information satisfied the agent, and he gave us a clean bill of health.

After the commotion caused by the drug scare died down, the morale in the camp immediately began to rise. We wished, of course, that we had never had to go through the whole experience, but perhaps it wasn't all bad. One fine young camper who witnessed this event later went on to be a high official in the FBI. He came up to me at a concert many years later and jokingly said, "Mr. S, everything I learned about my line of work I learned at Red Fox." All I can say is, "Thank you, Nurse Denny and Mrs. S for keeping America safe for us all!"

In December 1979 my mother died on after a short illness. I sold those beautiful fields and forests on the top of a small Berkshire mountain. Thus ended a wonderful part of my life, during which I had seen our tiny summer music school, which would enrich so many lives, grow and blossom into one of the more important music camps in the country. I lost two of the most important things in my world: Red Fox and my always supportive and loving mother. Every so often I return to visit those now empty grounds, as hundreds of former campers do, and I swear that I can still hear sound of music coming from the woods.

CHAPTER

30

LEONARD, NOT LENNY

About ten years before my mother's death and the closing of our beloved Red Fox, Leonard Slatkin and I both joined the Saint Louis Symphony. Leonard came to the Symphony as the new assistant conductor, and I as first cellist. Leonard's career with the Saint Louis Symphony, which started in 1968, was rather remarkable. For twenty-eight years, first as assistant conductor, then associate conductor, principal guest conductor, and finally as music director, Leonard profoundly affected the course of the Saint Louis Symphony.

He single-handedly brought what was already a great regional orchestra to the attention of the rest of the music world and kept it at the top, year after year, with his brilliant performances. With Leonard at the helm, we won umpteen Grammy nominations, made numerous international tours, had one of the best recording contracts in the business, and generally flourished. Leonard revolutionized the Symphony's audition process, which enabled us to draw some of the best candidates. Unlike some other music directors, he refused to pressure our ten-member audition committee into accepting his choices. His accomplishments were too numerous to quote, and we were grateful for all that he did.

The thing I am most grateful for is that he didn't fire me the day he became my boss. After the way some other know-it-alls and I treated him in his earlier years, it would have been understandable. Of course, we were nice to him, and we admired his great gift. But we were always giving him unsolicited advice, not out of lack of respect, but because of his humility and willingness to be one of us. "Hey, Lenny," someone would tell him, "your Sibelius symphony isn't cold enough." Or I might say, "Lenny, I think every conductor talks too much." (Just before I left the BSO, a friend said, "John, we will have to hire two cellists to replace you: one to play for you, and one to talk for you.")

I continued my advice to Leonard: "Why don't you be different from all the rest of the conductors and do everything with your stick?" He listened patiently to us mavens, until we really got obnoxious, and then he would answer, "Enough already. Just let me think about it for awhile." That was Lenny. He never got mad or held a grudge, no matter how obnoxious we were. His fuse was not long or short—he didn't have one.

Leonard Slatkin did not begin his illustrious stint with the Saint Louis Symphony with any grand ceremony. In fact, he made only one request to the orchestra before his first rehearsal as our new music director. He didn't ask directly, but made his preferences known through the personnel manager, almost as an aside.

"Lenny would like to be called Leonard," we were told. I believe this was in deference to Leonard Bernstein, whom he admired so much, and who was also known affectionately as Lenny. During that first rehearsal, we were all a little off balance, because no one wanted to be the first to call him Leonard, which seemed a bit cold. Besides, we didn't know Leonard yet. We had always worked with that quiet, calm, nice Lenny, and we were not sure what Lenny was going to be like now that he was Leonard and the big boss. The entire orchestra was tongue-tied, and since no one had the courage to address him by his new name, nobody could ask him a question about the music we were rehearsing. Leave it to our principal bass, Henry Loew, to think of the obvious. "Maestro, do you want us to be *piano* at letter B?" he asked from the back of the stage. There was silence, and Lenny—I mean Leonard—cocked his ear towards Henry and said, "Hey that sounds pretty good, could you say that maestro bit again?" The orchestra members howled, and Leonard and the Symphony were off to a great start. Leonard seemed just as nice as that old Lenny we once knew.

CHAPTER

31

MY, WHAT EARS HE HAS

Ormandy may have had "voodoo" eyes, which helped him work his "control-magic," but Leonard had an amazing set of ears, which enabled him to control everyone on the stage. To go along with these amazing ears, he had eyes that did not have to look at you to see what you were doing. This was an awesome combination, but what really topped it off was that his face never showed that he was hearing or seeing anything unusual. When he took some overt action, it always came as a shock. Leonard, unlike Ormandy, didn't appear to be looking at anyone, when in fact he was looking at everyone. With wide peripheral vision, he could conduct the woodwinds dead center in the orchestra, and still keep me, on his far right and almost in back of him, in his sight. How do I know? Because once during our early Saint Louis Symphony years, he did something that proved to me that he had eyes in the back of his head.

I was totally lost during a concert because my partner turned one of our pages too soon. This early turn robbed me of the opportunity to notice the correct number of bars of rest that I needed to count before my next entrance, and I saw disaster looming on the horizon. My stand-partner's body language told me that he was as much in the dark as I was, so he wasn't going to be any help. My body language, on the other hand, revealed nothing. If anyone was watching me at the time, they would have thought that I knew what I was doing. The last person I wanted to know that I had screwed up was Leonard, and I was sure he didn't notice me turn my head slightly to my right to catch the first activity from the cellists behind me, who always counted correctly.

Any activity back there would indicate that it was time for me to "lead" my section on the next entrance. I was going to fake my way through this blunder. This was an entrance for which Leonard had not previously given us a cue, and relying on the stand behind me was my only hope. One bar before my entrance, Leonard reached back, held up his index finger, and led me in by the nose, while still conducting the brass in the back risers. He never looked at me for a second. With the eyes in the back of his head, he must have seen me turn my head, and he thought, "John may need some help." This didn't happen just once.

On another occasion, in the middle of a rehearsal, I asked my stand-partner, Savely Schuster, a question, very softly, so as not to disturb Leonard, who was instructing our timpanist. After he finished his conversation with the percussionist, he turned and answered the question that I had meant for only Savely to hear. And this didn't happen just once. Very scary!

Leonard's magic ears and eyes made him the fastest rehearser in the business, and this was a great asset to us for many reasons. With Leonard's ability to quickly see and hear what needed fixing when preparing programs, we were able to cover more material in a shorter period of time than almost any other orchestra in the world. This, I'm sure, was a factor in our getting such wonderful recording contracts. The powers-that-be in the record industry knew that, with Leonard conducting us, we had a chance to produce more music per hour than previously thought possible, and in the recording business, time is money.

When it came to preparing contemporary music, no one could touch Leonard. Contemporary composers felt safe when he did their pieces because he could understand it when very few others could. Leonard could make even chaos sound good. His ears could quickly detect the incorrect chaos, enabling him to immediately turn it into correct chaos. Leonard has always championed American contemporary music, as he should, and I commend him for his willingness to do all that he can to support our composers. But his taste in modern music was definitely not mine. I was an old fogey when it came to some of that wild, off-the-wall, hot-off-the-press literature that Leonard came up with. Naturally I tried to keep that fact to myself, since telling your conductor that you really don't like his choice of repertoire isn't too smart. Whenever we played a contemporary piece that had a melody you could sing and a harmony that used some tonic and dominant chords, Leonard would turn to me and say, "John, this is modern music even you could love." I think that Leonard, besides having magic eyes and ears, was also a mind reader.

32

FAST, FASTER, FASTEST

When describing Leonard Slatkin's abilities, it's easy to make sweeping, but boring, statements. Leonard has a giant repertoire. Leonard is a great accompanist. Leonard conducts all music well, and in certain repertoire, he's the best. None of these attributes begins to capture some of the qualities I found most interesting about our former maestro. For one, Leonard rarely does anything exactly the same twice. I like to use the story of Moses on Mount Sinai as a way to illustrate Leonard's originality. It illustrates the differences I see in the way some conductors approach their art. Three maestros immediately come to mind who could portray, in my imagination, at least, the prophet quite well, but very differently.

Hans Vonk, the Saint Louis Symphony's music director in the nineties, would be most like the original. I could see Hans holding up the tablets after he has painstakingly removed every particle of dust from their surface, so that God's message to his people could be easily read and understood. He smiled when we got it. Franz Welser-Most, another great conductor with whom we had often worked, would, I imagine, bring everyone up to the mountain and make them cry so much for all their sins that a torrent of tears would clear away enough dust from the tablets to make them readable.

On the other hand, it seems to me that Leonard could dust off the Commandments and immediately head down the mountain, impressed with the message he's carrying, but already working on improving its delivery with an extra comma here, or perhaps a little bolder type there.

Leonard Slatkin knew how everything was supposed to go. He knew how "so and so," who spoke to Brahms in his sleep sixty years ago, did it, but hc was not interested in mimicking anyone. He belonged to the cult of the individual. I don't think that growing up with those two great musical parents, Eleanor and Felix Slatkin, who were the founders of the famous Hollywood String Quartet, among other things, ever did anything to make him doubt that it was OK to express himself in his own individual way. Leonard grew up surrounded with the likes of perhaps the greatest violinist in the world, Jascha Heifetz, the solo cellist Gregor Piatigorsky, and the famous movie composer Julius Korngold—all musicians who were not necessarily bound by tradition.

Often when Leonard was in one of his creative moods and he did something that was a little special, and I played my part by giving him what he wanted on the spur of the moment, a smile from him could make my evening. On the other hand, his experimentation didn't always work, and he knew it and said so.

Leonard Slatkin was good, and those magic eyes and ears told him so. But he was also a musician of great humility, and he would be the first to tell you, "I'm in process." He was always exploring, and pushing past the boundaries that the world tries to impose on us. Leonard could also push past the speed of sound, and the better the orchestra, the more he pushed.

The only other conductor under whom I have played who had that same—sometimes dangerous—fascination with speed was his namesake, Leonard Bernstein. Once during a Leonard Bernstein performance of Tchaikovsky's *Fifth Symphony* with the BSO, I sat on the "inside." The inside player is the one who must turn the pages for his stand-partner, and I could barely turn the pages fast enough to keep up with the music flying by. If it was speed you wanted, our Leonard could keep up with the other Leonard if he felt so inclined, and he did just that during "The Michigan Massacre" and "The Palm Desert Panic."

"The Michigan Massacre" is tied with "The Palm Desert Panic" for being the best examples of all-out, life-threatening speed during a concert. At a concert at the University of Michigan in Ann Arbor, the program consisted of works relatively unfamiliar to both the audience and the musicians. The musicians, of course, were a bit more familiar with the music than the audience. But the fact that we were facing three major works containing thousands of notes that didn't fit into patterns we normally saw was in itself mildly unsettling. Although that evening's pieces by Mennin, Schwantner, and Elgar were wonderful works in themselves, they were not then, and may never be, on any classical music lover's hit parade.

Perhaps that is why Leonard Slatkin decided to add a little extra dash to that particular performance. From the opening bell, we shot out of there like an antelope with a cheetah on its tail. The notes were flying by so fast that I was glad when I could get even six or seven out of the mandatory eight in a bar. Every time I thought that I had caught up with Leonard, he was a half bar ahead again. At first I was worried that some kind of rare disease was taking over my body and that, in my altered state, I thought that life was passing me by very quickly. A glance around the orchestra showed me that this was not so. Everyone was in trouble. Soon I began to believe the rumor that Leonard had to make a ten o'clock plane after the concert. But in spite of some tears from the younger players, who felt guilty for missing a few notes, the audience loved it. We old-timers were no longer alarmed over missing a few notes when Leonard was in his tornado mode.

In fact, some of my friends from the university told me that it was the most exciting concert that they had heard all year. That was Leonard. He knew when to apply the accelerator pedal and when not to, and he came off with one of the most exciting concerts imaginable. His batting average was fantastic, but once in a while even Babe Ruth fouled a ball into the stands, and I think that this was the case with "The Palm Desert Panic."

We should have known what was coming, because we were in the middle of a western tour, and the next night we were scheduled to play in Los Angeles, Leonard's hometown. He would often try to shake us up a little on the night before an important concert to help us be alert for those "creative moods" that he could get into during a special performance. As is often the case with Leonard, things are never the same; things are relative. Moments like those during "The Palm Desert Panic" can be fast, faster, and fastest, but they are never the same.

This time Leonard got to the starting line first and was gone before we could catch our breath. The speedometer was exciting to watch. Now he was half a beat ahead, now a whole beat; next he pushed it to one-and-a-half beats. All this time everyone was just trying to play together. There was no way one could play exactly with his beat, and he didn't want us to. He wanted to stay ahead of us all the time. Each orchestra musician must play a relative distance from the beat, but also exactly at the same time as everyone else in the orchestra. Keep in mind that each musician is hoping that he is making the same calculations, relative to Leonard's beat, that everyone else is making.

The most dangerous moment in this whole situation is when some musicians have a few measures rest. If they were to make their next entrance correctly, these resting musicians must carefully assess just how far the sound they were hearing from their colleagues was from Leonard's beat. "Let's see, that's the first beat I'm hearing from the violins, and Leonard is on the third beat, so I should be coming in right about now. Oops! Well, close. Better luck on the next one." If some players should be so reckless as to take their eyes off Leonard during these moments, they might as well pack up their instruments and get on our tour bus waiting in back of the hall. They'll never catch up with their friends again, let alone with Leonard.

The speedometer may have indicated that he was three beats ahead of us, for all I know, before that evening was over. As usual, the audience went wild. So did the orchestra. There were a lot of unhappy musicians, however, heading back to their hotel that night, and they complained to the maestro, who had always been accessible, that maybe this beating so far ahead of us was going a little too far. Leonard, who never seemed to get angry or defensive, simply told them, "I'm sorry, but tomorrow we play L.A. Remember?"

CHAPTER

33

NICE GUY

Leonard Slatkin is actually a nice guy. He's very reserved and not easy to really know, and I don't claim to, but he always seems ready to do a favor and expects nothing in return. He once flew all the way to my camp in New England, leaving behind his heavy Saint Louis Symphony schedule, to conduct my student orchestra at Red Fox. Besides conducting our kids, he played softball with them, and then ended up sleeping on a couch. In another instance, I was able to talk him into conducting at a music festival called Strings in the Mountains, which I had created in 1987 in Steamboat Springs, Colorado. He returned all his fees to the festival.

Leonard's pleasant nature and non-threatening demeanor make his orchestra feel at ease, and this is good for the music. One of my colleagues has called him the great facilitator, as Leonard often lets his musicians express themselves freely in the performances. Everyone feels safe with

Leonard, and thus he will get some pretty exuberant performances. Leonard would never dream of offending a musician in his orchestra, which is quite unusual for a conductor. A story I like to relate about him may show you how diplomatic he can be.

After the last rehearsal of Stravinsky's *Rite of Spring,* which Leonard conducted soon after he took over the reins of the Saint Louis Symphony, I noticed him sitting on a couch in the musicians' lounge reading a paper. As I walked by to retrieve my mail from the cubbyholes next to him, he said, without ever looking up, "John, you owe me an A flat." Puzzled by this accusation, I asked what he meant. He answered, "Go look at one bar before N in the last movement."

Running upstairs and onto the now empty stage, I found my part and opened to the page with the passage he mentioned. The note that he was talking about had a little handwritten zero above it, which indicated that it was a harmonic, but that would have produced an A natural. When I looked at the key signature, I could see why I owed Leonard an A flat. The zero was wrong, and though I hadn't put it on the page, I had obeyed it. So all that week Leonard, with those magic ears of his, had refrained from calling attention to my stupidity in front of the orchestra. Perhaps he hoped to run into me somewhere backstage and casually fix the problem.

Wasn't it lucky that when I went to get my mail, I just happened to bump into Leonard, reading his paper in the lounge, and he was able to correct my mistake privately. Just think what might have happened if Leonard hadn't accidentally gone to the musicians' lounge just before the concert that night.

Come to think of it, I never saw Leonard in that lounge again, and I rarely saw him with a newspaper unless he was doing a crossword puzzle. Nothing was ever an accident with Leonard.

CHAPTER

34

SIGNS, SIGNALS, AND MIXED MESSAGES

My life as an orchestra player, especially as a first cellist, depends on my getting a constant flow of the right information through clear signals that allow me to do my job properly. The conductor is the main source of most of this information, and he is often like a flight controller at a busy airport, as he listens and watches one hundred musicians sawing and tooting away on their instruments. He wants them to keep their original flight plan and not bump into each other as they travel across the many pages of the score. When we bump sometimes, he has to bring things to a halt and put us all into a holding pattern for a few moments until things get sorted out. This rarely happens, but even I was once so far off course that Ray Leppard had to bring the entire orchestra to a halt in order to save lives, but that comes later.

During a concert in which Leonard was conducting a very peaceful, quiet, and extremely beautiful rendition of the second movement of Dvořák's *New World Symphony,* I began to hear bumping and crashing coming from behind me. Leonard did not react at first, because he was probably hoping that the pilot in question was going to get his landing gear down in time, and all would be well. But the noise didn't stop; in fact, it got worse, as I heard a stand or two hit the deck. One of our bass players had been so moved by Leonard's interpretation that he keeled over in a dead faint. He wasn't hurt, but you can imagine the racket when a giant bass, bass stool, and its stand all start bouncing around during the pianissimo chords of the movement in question.

Leonard wisely put everyone in a holding pattern and stopped the orchestra as several doctors from the audience jumped up on the stage to carry off the dead-to-the-world musician and his precious bass. After the debris was cleared from the stage, Leonard manned the podium again, and we continued on as if nothing had happened. Everyone was delighted that our colleague had no injuries from the rather dramatic plunge that he had taken, but I think that I heard even more inquiries into the state of that valuable instrument, which, thank the Lord, was also unhurt.

This stopping and starting, which Leonard did during the Dvořák, was child's play, for he often had to send us much more complicated signals. Most composers take pity on the musicians and let them take a rest occasionally. But since everyone can't rest at the same time, or the audience will go home, the flight controller must often invite the idle players, resting in their holding patterns, to join the other musicians at exactly the right time. They do this, for example, by catching the anxious flutist's eye a moment before his entrance, looking at him with that "now or never" expression, and making a very slight hand motion in his direction. It's not polite to point unless you are standing on the podium, and then it is essential.

A conductor can't simply give everyone a cue every time he or she needs it, since the conductor doesn't have enough hands on his body to do this. Thus he has to make choices and concentrate on the most difficult entrances, like those after one hundred fifty bars rest, for example. Or he might choose the most important ones, which might be the re-entering of the violin section with the main theme. Everyone should be counting anyway, so what's the problem? I'll tell you. Have you ever been in a room with a hundred people who were able to stay focused for two hours without the tiniest lapse in their concentration, even for a split-second? That's all it takes. A tiny split second break, and terror takes over. "Let's see, was that the twenty-third or the twenty-fourth bar? Oh, my gosh, he's in two and I was counting in four. Let's see, if I multiply by two, I should come up with the proper number. That's right, forty-six!" About the time that you come up with the number forty-six, you notice that your colleagues are already playing bar forty-nine. When there are some lapses, it shows that we are only human.

A good conductor can see when you are in trouble and will alter his flight plan to give you a special cue if he thinks that you need it. I got very good, after a while, at letting Leonard know when I needed help. The slightly turned head I described previously worked quite well, and later I developed the slightly raised chin and adoring eyes routine that made the audience think I was admiring Leonard. In fact, I was asking for help. When this didn't work, I'd take up my bow ten or twelve bars too early and act as if I were about to crash in and destroy the mood. This always got his attention, and one of his hands would extend and gently shake a little, as if to say, "Wait!" Then I'd relax, follow his advice, and thank my lucky stars that the nice St. Bernard on the podium had found me frozen on the side of the mountain and was going to lead me in out of the cold.

Sometimes even the best conductor can't stop the inevitable. When a player is so sure of himself that he comes in wrong and doesn't hear the mess he's making, the conductor really starts to work overtime. First the maestro will try to be like a flagman on an aircraft carrier, waving off a plane trying to land on the pitching deck, and signaling it to come around again for another try. "You're too low, you're too low!" is not much different from "You're two bars too early, get out, you are ruining everything!" If the conductor can get the errant player's attention without having to throw the baton or scream, he can usually straighten him out without letting too many people in the audience know what's going on.

If his actual entrance hasn't come up yet, the maestro can usually insert the musician into his proper slot. If the actual entrance passed while the musicians were still blithely playing the right music in the wrong place, then the conductor's task is much harder. Sometimes it's better, I believe, to get rid of the musician temporarily, for all the trouble it's going to take to get him out and in again properly. Sometimes, however, it's not just one player who is meandering around in the wrong place during a live performance, but an entire platoon of musicians. When this happens it is a supreme challenge for even the best conductor.

I'm reminded of a memorable performance of Mahler's *First Symphony* by the Saint Louis Symphony under the direction of our then new music director, Hans Vonk. Before the evening was over, our maestro had to contend with twelve cellists who couldn't agree on where they should be making their contribution.

It had been a tough day for me. It was fun, exhilarating, enjoyable, but tough. I had rehearsals, concerts, and a three-hour stint behind a computer that took up every minute of my time. I was able to eat supper only because I was willing to hold a TV dinner on my lap while I drove to my evening symphony concert. The first moment I had to relax came during my last concert of the day, midway through the first movement of the Mahler when the cellos had a few bars rest before their next entrance. I sat back in my chair for a little respite from the task ahead of us, still counting to myself diligently. Noticing something in our music that I thought we should be aware of, I pointed out, with the tip of my bow, a particular spot on the page to Savely, my stand-partner, as a sort of reminder to ourselves of what was coming up. Savely thought that I was pointing to where we actually were in the music. For some strange reason I started to come to the same conclusion.

This probably happened because where I had pointed was a line of music below where we actually were, and the two lines looked exactly the same. In fact, they were the same except that where we should have been had six measures rest before our next entrance, and where I pointed to had only three. So three bars too early, Savely and I, quite confidently, started to play what we should have waited to play three bars later. This was a little two- and three-note motif that began on an F natural; then we had to slide down the fingerboard with one finger to an A, "Deeeeeeaah." Then the F was preceded by an E natural, but followed by another slide to that A, "De, Deeeeeeeeaaaah."

It happens that this figure, though very important, was not the melody, and even if it was played in the right place, it was supposed to sound slightly intrusive. The main action was taking place in the woodwind section, where Mahler was creating the sound of cuckoos. This, along with the fact that we couldn't see the shocked look on the faces of the rest of the cellists sitting behind us, was probably why we went on so long unaware of our error. Savely did wonder why the clarinet was in the wrong place, but he figured that that was the clarinet's problem, not his. A few bars later we again poured our hearts out with that three-note cello motif, again in the wrong place. It sounded good to me. In fact everything seemed to be going just fine, although I did notice something a little strange about our conductor. For the first time since I had been watching him conduct our concerts, the maestro was studying the music on his stand very intently. This was unlike him.

Usually Vonk was moving all over the podium, rarely even glancing at the score, but giving all his attention to every musician in the orchestra, gesturing enthusiastically to this player and that player to join him in his efforts to recreate what the composer intended. Now he was almost frozen. He was still beating with his right hand, but his left was searching the score for something. Of course, now we know that he was looking for some clue as to what his first stand of cellos was doing. His new posture should have alerted me, but it wasn't until I heard sliding noises from the rest of the cellists behind me that I suspected that something was amiss. Soon it sounded as if it were raining slides, and everyone had a different idea of where they should occur (reminiscent of the incident in Boston Symphony Hall). Our early entrance had confused my section.

Vonk raised his head, observed the mess in front of him and quickly started to direct traffic like he was in Bombay at a busy intersection that had to accommodate hundreds of bikes, buses, and cars entering from five different directions. First he waved me off, and then he started to unsnarl the main traffic jam. Though he wasn't saying a word with his mouth, he was talking to us with his eyes and face as well as his hands: "No, no, you over there, go away. Stop! Now you, yes you, stay right where you are. You in the back there, you're way behind." After about two minutes of extra work on the maestro's part, he was able to sort out the mess we'd created. During all of this the rest of the musicians just played what they were supposed to, with gentle smiles on their faces.

Finally the torture ended, and we were back on track. The rest of the symphony was played stunningly by all, and the orchestra and Maestro Vonk received a standing ovation. Because of the peculiar nature of the music at the moment we erred, few, if any, in the audience noticed anything amiss. Besides, as I stated earlier, an occasional flaw only enhances the rest of our perfect performances.

Savely and I apologized after the concert to our conductor, who graciously forgave us. I thought that the whole thing was over and done with, but the next evening, when I was entering our concert hall for our repeat performance, I swear that I heard our infamous three-note tune from the Mahler symphony emanating from the men's dressing room. Instead of "Deeeeeeeeaaaah" I heard my colleagues singing, "Lawwwwwwwwwwost. We're lawwwwwwwwwost. Please he111111111p us."

35

COULD YOU BE A LITTLE CLEARER, PLEASE?

With so much at risk in this business, conductor usually tries to be very clear about what he intends for us to do. Otherwise we won't do what he intends. Henryk Szeryng was an example of the opposite approach. He was a great violinist, who was often understated in his playing and conducting.

After one very successful Bach violin concerto performance with us in which he both conducted the orchestra and played the solo part, he came out to acknowledge the audience's approval. Then he turned to me, bowed, and extended his hand to thank me, I thought, for the few cello solos in the part that I had just played with him. I graciously returned his bow. Szeryng stepped a few feet closer and bowed to me again, drawing another gracious bow from me. He stepped even closer and once more bowed even deeper to the floor with that strange extended right hand. Remembering the embarrassing Ormandy incident, I started to ask myself, "Is there a message here I'm not getting?"

Szeryng then stood right next to me, and this next bow was going to leave two musicians with sore heads if we weren't careful. With his head almost in my stomach, I finally heard what he had been muttering ever since he started all this bowing. Apparently Henryk had been anxious to play an encore for his adoring public, but couldn't get on with it until he could get us back in our seats. For some reason he thought that if he could get me to sit down, everyone else would follow. So he had not been congratulating me; he had been saying, "Sit down!" I finally did.

Understatement in conducting is dangerous, but vagueness is worse. More than once I have been sucked into an "ambush" by a conductor's vague beat. One of the best examples of the horrendous sound a conductor's vague beating can elicit from a musical instrument occurred on tour with Walter Susskind conducting Tchaikovsky's *Fifth Symphony.*

Each night Walter was getting a little vaguer as he approached the last chords of the cadence before the coda in the finale. It was almost as though he was off in a dream somewhere, and he gave those all-important beats as if they were just afterthoughts. The tricky spot needed a more definite gesture from the conductor than what he gave that evening if it were to have any chance of sounding like what the composer intended. That's the spot where the audience often claps because of the giant pause after the loud chords in question are over. When the audience hears only silence for a few seconds, it mistakenly thinks the piece is over. A very fine violinist's career almost ended after he understandably got confused at this point in the music. The rest of the orchestra had been through this kind of confusing situation before, and the vaguer Susskind got, the more everyone just ignored him and stuck together like elk in a winter storm.

Unfortunately, during this concert, the violinist in question was seated in such a way that he couldn't pick up on what was happening with the rest of us, and he strayed from the herd. When we reached that now famous spot, he misread what the maestro was vaguely indicating and played a huge fortissimo in a rest, while the remainder of the orchestra huddled together on the sidelines. Now that's really all that happened, and there's not much more that you can say about it, except that for more than twenty years, people have been trying to describe exactly what the dreadful noise, which the well-meaning violinist produced, was like. First you have to understand that this sound almost never made it to the outside world. When this player put his bow on the strings, with fifty pounds of arm weight about to be applied to the instrument, he noticed that he might be misreading the signals coming his way. So he tried to stop. If he had succeeded, we would have one less marvelous story to tell. We're grateful that didn't happen.

What did happen, though, was that he was able to stop most of the lateral motion as his bow arm locked. There wasn't much that he could do about the fifty pounds of arm weight that were already pressing into his strings. It was this unintentional, but unrelenting, arm weight that produced the unique sound that has never been duplicated to this day. Some have likened it to the sound of a wooden crate being crushed by a three hundred-pound man, others to the cracking sound of a giant redwood tree as it begins to fall to the forest floor. All these sound qualities were definitely present. There is a general consensus, however, that the only way you could even get close to that famous horrible sound would be if you took one healthy cat, with good vocal chords, stretched him ten to fifteen feet from end-to-end, and then recorded, on tape, the cat's reaction. If you slowed down this recording of the cat screeching to about half speed, you might then get very close to the pitch and intensity of that unintentional solo in Tchaikovsky's *Fifth Symphony*.

CHAPTER

36

LOST

It has become obvious to me, after playing in professional symphony orchestras for so long, that for a conductor to be most effective in his work, he should give clear, direct signals. Understatement is not good. Vagueness is worse and can be quite dangerous. The only thing worse than vague beating by a conductor is wrong beating, and there can be hell to pay if things don't get straightened out fast. There are two ways a conductor can deal with this problem of wrong beating or, as it is more commonly called, a mistake.

Here Leonard Slatkin is a master. Every conductor occasionally makes mistakes, and his musicians rarely judge him harshly for them. When Leonard slipped up for a second, he recognized it immediately, maybe even smiled slightly to let everyone know that he knew that he did, and now he knew that we knew that he knew that he did. The smile is like a signal, which says,

"Ignore what just happened and carry on without me until I get my bearings." It works every time, and we never worried about Leonard with even the most complicated scores. He would always get us out alive, no matter what. I call this the "humble-acceptance" technique. There is another approach that has several names, but it is not half as effective. It is, however, far more entertaining. Probably the best name we could use here is the "macho-bluff" technique. It could also be called the "it's not my problem, you have to find me" technique.

The most wonderful example that I remember of this "macho-bluff" technique was during a performance of Stravinsky's *Rite of Spring* at Tanglewood in the sixties, with Eleazar De Carvalho conducting—by memory. De Carvalho was very impressive conducting this music, and it was quite a feat for someone to even conduct this incredibly difficult and complicated piece, with tricky rhythmic patterns and constantly changing time signatures, let alone do it by memory. Well, that night, in front of ten thousand people in the shed and on the Tanglewood lawns, he almost brought it off, and I was quite impressed. What most impressed me was how skilled he was at using the "macho-bluff "technique. I swear that not one person in the audience knew that he was employing it, and I'm not sure that he didn't fool a few of us in the orchestra too. Everything was going fine until we got to the last movement and he slipped an extra beat into a three beat bar, or something like that. To be honest, I can't remember exactly what he did, but it definitely was not what Stravinsky indicated.

Everyone can make a mistake, but not everyone can carry it off like he did. He did not smile or change course, so most of us didn't know for sure what was happening. In a piece as complicated as that, you are spending a good deal of time with your head buried in your music, counting for all you're worth.

As we glanced up from the page every so often, we began to notice that he wasn't where we thought he should be. The music was still pounding away in a fairly orderly fashion, and we tried to ignore him for a while. At first I wasn't sure who was wrong, but a glance around the orchestra told me that something was up and a lot of other players were as confused as I was. Even Joey Silverstein, our concertmaster, who never made a mistake and took things quite seriously, was beginning to smile. I knew immediately what was happening. We were witnessing one of the greatest displays of the "macho-bluff" technique in recent history. He was lost, and we were lost, but at least half the orchestra didn't realize it at first, and the audience certainly didn't and never would.

A dead giveaway should have been the change we were hearing that occurred in the famous brutal rhythmic motif that went dadum, (rest) dadum, dadum, (rest) dadum, dadum dadum. Because no two people were in the same place at the same time, someone was always playing in every rest. The rhythm was just one endless dadum, dadum, dadum, dadum, ad infinitum. The spaces were gone. I looked over at my stand-partner and saw that he was still concentrating intently on the music in front of us and was unaware, like so many others in the orchestra, that we were creating chaos, not music. We had another page to go, but I turned it early to get his attention. He looked at me in shock, and then I jerked my head towards the rest of our confused colleagues in an effort to get him to look around the orchestra and see what was happening. Soon he was smiling and chopping away randomly with his bow, like the rest of us. All this time, our maestro was gesturing dramatically, bringing in imaginary forces here and there, and pulling off one of the best demonstrations of the "macho-bluff" technique I have ever seen.

One reason I had already turned the page was because there was a big fermata (pause) near the top of our music, and I thought that the whole orchestra might sooner or later use it to gather its forces and regain its equilibrium. At a time like this, it didn't hurt to be too early. This "hill," where the music paused for a moment and the musicians could group to make one last stand against the forces of confusion, was preceded by some ascending scales up to it from different parts of the orchestra.

This, I knew, would be a good signal for us that our place of refuge was fast approaching. I stayed on the look-out, and sure enough, we soon began to hear different groups start their scales on their last ascent to the famous fermata. De Carvalho, without coming out of his pose for a moment, picked up on what was happening and began herding the rest of the orchestra up the hill to safety. Now, we didn't get there all at the same time, but we didn't leave that hill until every musician had ascended and parked himself on a G sharp diminished chord and had time to catch his breath. We had made it, and there was a good chance that we were saved because we were all together now. If the maestro could avoid repeating his previous error, we would make it to the end without another mishap, and that's important, because an orchestra that plays together, stays together and usually has a good chance of ending together. Ending together was all we were asking for at this point.

Unfortunately our brave conductor repeated his previous error, and soon everyone was again frantically searching for another waterhole somewhere between where we were and the end of the piece. Today I can't honestly remember who saved us. Probably some brass players, who had

had enough of this nonsense and blasted out their parts so loudly that we all, including our conductor, had to follow or be left behind. However it happened, we all got together by the final bell, and all is well that ends well. The audience loved it. Why not? There must be a million notes in that great Stravinsky masterpiece, and we misplaced only fifty or sixty thousand of them. And through it all, De Carvalho faultlessly displayed the "macho-bluff" technique. We were very proud of our director that evening, but to be honest, I still think the "humble-acceptance" technique is a lot easier on the musicians.

CHAPTER

37

A DIFFERENCE OF OPINION

Sometimes a conductor has the best of intentions, but still ends up confusing half the orchestra with his signals. It would take instant replay and a three-man referee board made up of an impartial conductor, a musician from another orchestra, and a Supreme Court judge to determine who was at fault. In my many years of watching conductors from my chair in Powell Hall, I have seen them throw us lots of curves that we could not figure out.

During an exuberant performance of Tchaikovsky's *Sixth Symphony*, one half of the Saint Louis Symphony was at odds with the other half. We stayed that way for quite a while. The winds and brass had picked the second half of the measure, and I believe that the strings chose the first half. It was a very interesting sound, but its appeal was limited, and soon the brass won the battle for supremacy, as they usually do. They are among the loudest members of our "family" and can be bullies in these situations. Only the timpanist, the king of the jungle in the loud department, is more powerful, but like the lion, he rests a lot. It would be completely out of place for him to come to the rescue if he has nothing to play at the moment. He usually lets everyone work it out on his own.

Whose fault was it? After that Tchaikovsky debacle, there was plenty of blame to go around, but the general consensus was that it had to be the conductor's fault. An impartial observer might question that, however, and ask, "How come half of you saw one thing and the other half saw something else?" I would say that this conductor's "control-magic" got short-circuited, and he zapped himself instead of us.

CHAPTER

38

VERDI, JOHN, VERDI!

Signs and signals don't always have to originate from the podium to be of help. When I first got into the BSO, I got a signal from a principal in another section. I still remember this fifty years later. The principal violist, Joseph de Pasquale, was Italian-American. So am I. It meant that, as the older member of the "family," he felt that he had a responsibility to signal me when he observed that, back there on the last stand of the cellos, I was not using enough vibrato. To this day I can still see that massive, handsome face staring at me as he shook his left hand wildly. I got the message and have been trying to keep the vibrato going ever since.

There's many a time when one colleague will signal his stand-partner by unobtrusively holding a finger down by the side of his chair to prevent him from entering early. Counting accurately during rests to avoid this is always a challenge, and I have used the "double protection" method myself. With my left hand behind the cello so that you couldn't see my insecurity, I counted on those five fingers as well as in my head. In rehearsal, even this sometimes fails because you might lose your concentration while you change a mark in your part. I always half turned to the woman behind me, Cathy Lehr, who we all knew never miscounted, and she would give me a high-five, again, unobtrusively, by the neck of her cello, when five, fifteen, or twenty-five came up.

The Saint Louis Symphony is made up of some of the nicest people in the world. They would always do anything they could to help you. For instance, if there was a way that they could warn you that you were about to drive off a cliff, they wouldn't hesitate to send some signal to save your life. The musicians in the Saint Louis Symphony are often as protective of each other as mothers are of their young children. But sometimes even the best mothers get momentarily distracted, and their babies get away from them and start walking enthusiastically into a busy street. One Saturday evening in Powell Symphony Hall, I was the "baby," and there was a two-ton truck barreling down the highway straight at me.

On the night of this accident, I was preoccupied with a new bow that I was considering purchasing. I had walked out onto the stage before the concert to warm up with it. This is not unusual in itself as most American orchestras straggle onto the stage fifteen to twenty minutes before the concert begins so that the musicians can warm up and be ready to go when the baton comes down. There were a few cello solos in the Verdi *Te Deum,* which we were playing that evening, and I wanted to see how they sounded with this new bow. Putting the Verdi on the stand, I quietly warmed up. In a little while, a stage manager came up to me and said, "John, we are starting the program with some a cappella songs, so the orchestra has to get off the stage until the second piece on the program."

After some beautiful choral singing, the orchestra trailed onto the stage for the next number. My brilliant stand-partner, Savely Schuster, rushed in at the last minute to take his seat next to mine. He had just come from playing three chess games in the musicians' lounge, and I don't think he was any more alive to the moment than I was. I'll have to admit here that I distracted him from his first responsibility as the inside player, which was to make order of the chaos on our stand and put the piece of music that we were about to play where we could see it. Instead, I immediately and selfishly grabbed his attention by asking him to listen carefully to my sound in my upcoming solos during the Verdi, which we were, I assumed, about to play. I told him that I wanted to know how my new bow responded.

Then, before we realized it, Ray Leppard was on the podium. I had been so busy talking that I didn't even see Ray come out, and as I turned away from Savely, I saw that the maestro was giving us a very slow, clear, downbeat. Savely and I raised our bows, took a quick glance at the music on the stand, which was the Verdi that I had been looking at before the stage manager had asked me to leave, and prepared to give him a huge fortissimo chord, which was clearly printed on the first page.

Just before I struck those two strings with all my might, I had a thought that should have made me hesitate: "Why were the violins just sitting there and not raising their bows to begin this Verdi masterpiece too?" My stand-partner had that same thought and several more. (He's quite bright.) He started asking himself some more important questions: "Where is the chorus? They sing this piece with us, don't they?" This really opened his mind to other possibilities: "Maybe we don't play the Verdi yet. Maybe we are supposed to be playing something else first."

Savely stopped his bow a half inch above the strings and was just about to signal me in some way to stop also. Unfortunately the "baby" had already stepped off the curb, and Savely's good thinking took too much time. By now, my bad thinking was in complete control of my hands and arms: "You are the principal, do your job, lead your section." Feeling a little like I was leading the

"Charge of the Light Brigade," I ripped into the fortissimo chord with all the force I could bring to bear on my cello. The two recording engineers in the radio booth upstairs had their sound levels set for a triple pianissimo entrance from the cellos, since they were under the impression that we were playing the serene *Notturno for Strings* by Dvořák, not the more bombastic Verdi for full orchestra and chorus. My chord, apparently, almost took out their eardrums. After ripping off their earphones, I was told later, they fell on the floor, howling with laughter.

Now, it didn't take anyone too long to figure out what had happened, but at this point, unless you were actually watching me, you might not have known that I was the culprit who had created that explosion. Ray immediately stopped the orchestra, and we all froze. I sent an ESP message, special delivery, to Savely: "Don't touch the music." The Dvořák, which we should have been playing, begins quietly on an F sharp and later goes on for twenty-eight bars on another F sharp. I thought, "Now all we have to do is play that F sharp until the audience's attention is somewhere else, and then we can make the switch and no one will be able to pin this thing on me." Too late.

Either Savely's receiver wasn't on or I sent the message to the wrong address. In front of two thousand people in the audience and, worse, sixty of my colleagues, Savely started rummaging around our music stand looking for the right music, as Ray tapped his foot impatiently. Everyone was now aware of who had just made that terrible noise, and I was as red as a beet. Not a soul looked at us. When we finished, I could hear quiet snickering, and I saw orchestra members looking at each other and smiling. For a brief moment, everyone was considerate of our feelings and no one said a word. Then, from the back of the viola section, I heard Moe Jacobs call out loudly enough for half the orchestra to hear, "Hey, Savely, what's the next piece?"

It's been many years since that mistake, but no one would let me forget it. Whenever I asked, "What are we playing next," they would all shout, "Verdi, John, Verdi!"

CHAPTER

39

EYE OF THE STORM

Oh, give me a break! In the last fifty years I've
played well over ten thousand concerts. Ninety-
nine percent of the time I was boring: I played the
right music on the right part of the page and
counted the right number of bars. Show me a
hitter with a better batting average. So, be fair.
Believe me when I tell you that I was not always
as spacey as I was that Verdi evening. Usually my
colleagues and I were incredibly focused. The
magnetism of most of our conductors as well as
their abundant supply of "control-magic" would
not allow us to be anywhere but in the moment.
Once the glorious sound that one hundred
musicians can produce began to surround us, we
were not going anywhere but in the direction that
our maestro mapped out for us.

After an incredible Saint Louis Symphony
performance of Shostakovich's *Sixth Symphony,*
conducted by Franz Welser-Most, a listener,
moved by the performance, asked what it was like

to be in the center of that sound. I just love questions like that. When you have just returned from an exciting journey, there is nothing more satisfying than sharing with others what you've experienced. During a concert, if you seem to transcend yourself and enter a land that is rarely seen, it is important not to let that slip from your memory. Besides, it's great to pontificate in front of someone who has actually asked for it.

What was it like? There is no simple answer. If you took a trip through Europe, your feelings could change depending on which country you were visiting at the time. As you move through a great symphony like the Shostakovich *Sixth Symphony*, you encounter different musical expressions on every page. Each group of notes that the composer collects and shapes for your pleasure creates different sensations within your consciousness.

For example, the brilliant *Presto Finale* of Shostakovich's symphony was like riding the back of a great white shark that's twisting and turning as it races through the depths of the ocean. If you didn't hang on tightly, you were history. Franz drove us at a whirlwind tempo, and the ferocity of the sound he demanded was, as he would often say in rehearsals, over the top. "Ladies and gentlemen, I want you to go over the top here." If you faltered for a second and missed the alternating rhythmic patterns that Shostakovich cleverly inserted into his music, you were in danger of being swallowed alive, or noticed by the conductor, which was just as dangerous. At the maestro's tempo, five bars would flash by in a mini-second, and finding yourself out of sync with one hundred of your colleagues for even half a second could be embarrassing. Once you are out of sync, it is extremely hard to rejoin the group.

At that concert we were all running on maximum power, and yet he was asking for more. My cello was in danger of being sawed in two. The previous evening, on one of my brutal up-bow swipes, I accidentally hooked the frog of my bow on the A string, ripping it out of my hand and sending it skyward. A desperate grab with my left hand captured only air, as my bow crashed to the stage, turning all heads in my direction. As I awkwardly reached over to retrieve it from the floor, right under the conductor's nose, I thought, "Maybe I'm getting too carried away here."

This evening the intensity level was again heading towards the self-destruct mark just as we arrived at the final chords, which brought the entire audience leaping to its feet. The audience was happy, I'm sure, to see that we had made it out of there alive.

The first movement, which seemed to encompass all the sadness and hopelessness of the Russian people during the reign of the Red Terror in the 1930s, left us chilled to the bone. It didn't help that the maestro appeared to be crying. He forced us to endure every nuance of pain that

Shostakovich described in his music. "What was it like?" the listener had asked. It was unbelievable.

Our tuba player, Mike Sanders, came up to me in the dressing room after the performance and asked, "Was that as good as I thought it was?" It was. A more interesting question would be, how did Franz draw from us such an astounding performance for even as great an orchestra as the Saint Louis Symphony? How did it happen?

CHAPTER

40

GHOSTS

My theory is that Franz Welser-Most cleverly planned his strategy for those performances that drove the audiences wild long before he arrived in St. Louis. It was that old "control-magic" at work again. I'm sure of it!

Franz relied on ghosts. He brought the composer back from the hereafter and sat him down in a chair next to him as he began to study the score, which he took in almost intravenously. When the maestro arrived for the first rehearsal, he started slowly building for the performance three days away. He was very friendly during breaks, not going off to his private room to rest, but spending time talking warmly with the musicians and renewing friendships from previous guest appearances. This was important for Franz in his efforts to control the orchestra, because he knew that he was soon going to ask a lot of us. It might even be considered beyond the call of duty, and he wanted us to be comfortable with him before we got too far. After all, he was going to take us near dangerous cliffs and noisy battlefields. We had to like and trust him enough to stick very close, or we were not going to pull it off.

Franz Welser-Most's first rehearsal might have been called a bit tedious, because he was unrelenting in his efforts to get us to feel what he did about the music. He would make us play passages over and over, and just when we thought that we had gotten whatever he wanted, he did it again "for the last time." Don't believe him. Sometimes one note wouldn't be dark enough, and he would start dictating just how we were to move our bows and exactly what part of the bows should have touched the strings. The first rehearsals were filled with long explanations of what the composer meant with this note or that phrase. Pretty soon, we couldn't play it any other way than the way he demanded. We couldn't even defy him, if we were foolish enough to try. The magic had just begun to take its effect. Finally, during the last of our usual four rehearsals, things began to flow easier, and we started getting anxious to see how all this work was going to play out in the concert.

The night of the performance, the maestro walked out to the podium, waited a few seconds for the spirit of Shostakovich to take over his body, and then began the voyage no one would forget. From the first notes of the dark viola and cello theme, you could see Franz was in Russia somewhere, and to our amazement, we were all following him there. It was hard to keep your eyes off him. Now he was crying. He felt the pain of all Russia, and we felt it too. He had us in his spell. We were convinced that he was sincere, so what else could we do but give him one hundred fifty percent. This was not a time to be cynical.

Now something new happened. He was going forward, no longer holding us back. That control he had over us was still there, but he used it to pull more out of us than we knew existed. During the last two fast movements, he conducted with more abandon and became almost reckless. We stuck with him. We may have hung on for dear life, but it was exciting. His sincerity, combined with the focus he brought to the task at hand, made us feel that he knew what he was doing, and he successfully negotiated all the tricky bends coming up on the road that we were speeding down. He relaxed for just a second and smiled at a little flourish that I gave to a fast two-note, almost humorous cello motif in the midst of this excitement. But only for a second. Then it was back to concentrating on the extraordinary performance, as we rushed to the emotional finale.

That's how he did it. He played on our emotions. He took advantage of us. Franz shrewdly planned all along to get us to the point that we couldn't help ourselves, and our emotions would make us do something for him and the music that we might never have done otherwise, thus the earthshaking performance. That's my theory, and I know I'm right. Maybe I should have asked him about it when he came for his next guest appearance with us. But maybe we shouldn't bother a magician like that.

CHAPTER

41

ORCHESTRA-WATCHING

Orchestra-watching is very similar to bird-watching. You have to find their habitat, sit down, be still, and quietly observe. You should not make noise, such as coughing, which will disturb your quarry, especially that big bird on the podium. As a boy I used to love watching all those interesting birds warm up. I was watching those who were already doing what I hoped to do someday.

I always thought that I could tell a lot about the musicians before the conductor ever gave the downbeat. It was fun to build psychological profiles of the musicians based on my preconcert observations. When a player came onto the stage at the last minute, not having looked at the music like that other fellow who was out on the stage for ten minutes sawing away, I came to a conclusion that was probably as wrong then as it would be today.

My former stand-partner, Savely Schuster, was a case in point. Savely memorized very quickly and grasped concepts immediately. He is what we would call a "quick study." Sometimes he would sit there staring at music that I was chopping away at, and though he was not moving a muscle, he was practicing it just like everyone else. He simply didn't need to do it physically to imbed it mentally. I've seen him do some astonishing things when the spirit moved him.

For example, during rehearsals, while part of the orchestra was resting and the conductor was working with the first violins on some particularly difficult technical passage, he would amuse himself and me by playing the passage perfectly in tune with the violins. He played it very softly so as not to irritate the conductor or make the violinists feel badly. What he was doing was three times as hard as what they were doing. To match the violin pitch, he had to play it so high, up close to the bridge of the cello, that he got rosin all over his fingers. With all this talent and brilliance, he never showed off. Sometimes I forgot who I was sitting next to. Savely didn't need to cram as I did, so don't be fooled by late arrivers.

It was fascinating to me, when I first started going to concerts, to try to figure out what kind of person each musician was. I would observe their social skills as the musicians interacted with each other before and after the concert began. While one player might be deeply engrossed in preparing a tricky section of the music, his stand-partner might plop down next to him and start bending his ear. Sometimes you need good bird-watching binoculars to catch the subtleties here, but I thought you could learn an awful lot from what would happen next. The totally insensitive player would keep sawing away and occasionally nod his head a little to acknowledge that someone was bothering him while he practiced. The real gentleman, like our concertmaster, David Halen, would instantly stop his work and talk to you, as if you were the only person left on earth. I was somewhere in the middle and would turn to the person talking to me, smile, nod, and even answer some question, but I continue playing.

Once the downbeat occurs, you should see sixty bows moving so well in sync that they remind you of wild geese rising to fly south. You need those binoculars to catch the little things that start to happen. One might notice a flicker of a smile here and there, when inside jokes are being played out. My stand-partner and I would often try to second-guess what left-hand fingering the other was going to use during a romantic phrase for the cellos. If we both opted to do the same juicy slide up to a note on the G string at the same time, a little grin might appear on my partner's face that only my fairly good peripheral vision could detect.

If you manage to become an advanced orchestra-watcher, after many years of quiet observation and study you may start noticing some things that will slip by the average concertgoer. For example, I used to love to see if all the violinists were playing in the same part of the bow as their concertmaster, because it makes the sound more uniform. Or were the left hands of the cellists all placed on the same part of their fingerboards? This isn't always necessary because there are several acceptable ways to finger every passage. You will need those binoculars to see if the winds are breathing together on their melodies, which they usually should be. There is no end of things to observe.

The way that principal strings lead their sections in after rests are always fun to see. My favorite leader to watch when I first started observing was, without question, Joe de Pasquale, who looked every bit like a cavalry officer about to lead his troops into battle. A few beats before the violas were to enter, he would slowly and grandly raise his bow high in the air like a sword, waving it ever so slightly, and let his arm descend even more slowly to the instrument, exploding in a fury of bow movements the instant he touched the string. The culmination of this gesture would occur exactly when the violas were to play their first note. A classic example of this was the first viola entrance in Berlioz's *Romeo and Juliet*. My friends, who were in awe of Joe, would just turn to me and silently mouth "charge" after he successfully brought in his section.

This approach had some risk attached to it because you could look awfully silly if you miscounted. That's why some principals use the "safe sneak" method. If your addition is wrong, you don't draw too much attention to yourself. My style is a little of both. I lean toward one or the other method depending on how confident I feel that day.

One of the greatest section leaders of all time was the incomparable Sammy Mayes, the solo cellist of the Boston Symphony and also, at two different times, the first cellist of the Philadelphia Orchestra. He was to an orchestra what a prima ballerina is to the ballet. For me, watching his beautiful movements was so satisfying that my eyes would stay riveted on him the entire program. You could just see the music flowing through his arms to reach us way in the back of the hall. During rehearsals after I had joined the BSO, he would show off his incredible gift for mimicry by humorously imitating everyone in the section. Just before I left the BSO, I remember thinking, "If I ever become a first cellist, I will try to give as much of myself to the performances as Sammy did."

Another amazing action on the stage that you can pin your bird-watching binoculars on is the one that the oboes, clarinets, and bassoons indulge in as they set up housecleaning in the middle of the stage during the concert and still manage to keep track of where they are in the music. Besides constantly mopping out the insides of their instruments, the oboes also have to run a woodworking shop. They seem to be carving away at their reeds during every bar's rest that they have in the music. All of the winds are constantly dissembling and assembling their horns during the performance to make us nervous. Somehow they always get them back together again just before they have to play. With all this extracurricular activity, they still come in on time. This is very impressive to me since I know that they can't possibly use my finger-counting method.

There is no question that it can be as illuminating to see the musicians as it is to hear them. If you could have watched me several years ago during an Opera Theatre of St. Louis performance, I know that you could have put together a fairly accurate psychological profile after observing me for only a minute.

It was 7:00 P.M. on a lazy Sunday, and I was enjoying a light supper on our screened-in porch when the phone rang. I almost ignored it because I needed to dress for an 8:00 P.M. opera performance that the Saint Louis Symphony was to play that night. On my way upstairs, I picked up the phone and was surprised to hear, coming very clearly out of the earpiece, the music from the very same opera that I was to play in an hour.

"John, where are you?" asked Joe Kleeman, our associate personnel manager. Slamming the phone down, I dashed out of the house, carrying some of my clothes and my cello. I got into that racecar that I thought I had left in Massachusetts. Dressing as I drove, I tried to figure out where I had gone wrong. This was the first opera of the season, and I had been out the summer before with an arm injury. I either forgot that the opera was at 7:00, not 8:00, or they had moved the time of the opera performance while I was gone. Rehearsing an excuse was not as important right now as the fact that I had a big solo about twenty-two minutes into the opera. Here I was, racing around those back roads in Webster Groves, and it was already twelve minutes after the hour.

As I pulled into the musicians' parking lot, the time was 7:17 P.M. When I flew down the stairs to the room next to the orchestra pit, it was going on 7:20. With my cello out of its case, I tried to enter the crowded pit, but Roland Pandolfi, our first horn at the time, waved me off like one of those aircraft carrier signalmen. His seat was right at the entrance where I needed to go. He was in the middle of a solo, and the last thing he needed was a late cellist climbing on top of him.

The music was swelling and the time for my beautiful solo fast approached, but I had no way into the orchestra pit. Seeing the stage manager at the other end of the room, I yelled, "Hey, Leroy, how can I get in there? I've got a solo in exactly sixty seconds." He quickly took me to a hall under the stage and showed me a side door right under the cello section. With half a minute to go, I squeezed through the door and motioned to my assistant, Cathy, that I was coming up. She was in my chair and ready to play "my" solo. She graciously moved back to her chair, and I slid into my seat with about three bars to go before I had to play. As the conductor gave me the cue, he did a double take because he was pretty sure he hadn't seen me there before.

The solo went well. But what's more important is that now you should easily be able to put together a psychological profile of me. You would need only to have witnessed those last thirty seconds, when I emerged from that side door and pushed my way through the rest of the orchestra to get to my seat, to draw your conclusions:

1. Slightly disorganized and doesn't read schedules.
2. Moves fast and is resourceful in tight spots.
3. Is excessively possessive about his solos and will kill before letting anyone else play them.

CHAPTER

42

ON TEACHING YOUR OWN CHILDREN:

DON'T! WELL, MAYBE

"It was the best of times, it was the worst of times"—Dickens had it right. When it came to teaching my own children, it was both.

It must have been hard for my kids to endure my shouting up the stairs, "You are flat. Play it again and slowly," all those years, but it wasn't easy on me either. After years of some severe teaching by my father, I was determined to be the most patient, loving, supportive, understanding, long-suffering parent-teacher who ever put a violin, viola, or cello in his innocent children's hands. That's why I took it as such a personal defeat when I would calmly make a point to my kids during a lesson and my wife, Peg, would yell, "John, if that screaming doesn't stop, I'm going to call the police." It really wasn't fair, because I always started out so well, but my kids took advantage of me. Remembering how tough it had been for me at times, and not wanting to be an oppressive father, I always approached the lessons with a light heart and a big smile. My kids, on the other hand, were thinking to themselves, "Here comes Mr. Nice Guy. I'll give him twenty minutes of sass, he'll blow up, and Mom will get me out of here." I would say, "Steffy, please play that etude from Letter B and please, very slowly this time, sweetheart." She, of course, would start playing it fast, while muttering under her breath, "Oh Daddy, you don't know anything." Since I was a cellist and she was a violinist, she wasn't too far off, but just about thirty minutes of this lip did it every time, and I would hit the ceiling. Her mom would intervene, I would feel bad, and Steffy was home free.

Sometimes I would try the stay-calm-but-be-dramatic approach. Keeping my voice very low and quiet, I would try to do something to shock her into changing her attitude. I saw my fatherly appeals going nowhere. Once, after she didn't seem to be putting much effort into her lessons, I said, "If you don't want to play the violin, let's just throw it away," and I took her violin and tossed it with a great flourish onto her bed, where I thought it would land safely. It hit the bed, but didn't stop traveling. Continuing its journey it bounced off the nice soft mattress and made a crash landing on the hard floor. Neither the violin nor I looked too good after that experience.

Sara, my cellist daughter and presently a founding member of the Eroica Trio, had a more direct approach. If I entered her room to make a suggestion about how she was practicing, she'd just stick her bow in my tummy, push me towards the door, and say, "Thanks, Dad. You told me that yesterday; it doesn't work. Good-bye." This always surprised me so much that I didn't know how to react, and I wasn't quite sure who was teaching whom. Somehow we limped through.

Steffy eventually got a wonderful violin teacher, Eiko Kataoka, a violinist and colleague of mine in the Saint Louis Symphony, and Sara learned by osmosis. She was hearing me practicing all the pieces she was to play and never got too many lessons. My patience finally did improve. I even got smart enough to find something else to do and stayed out of the house when they practiced. They would occasionally try to suck me into the old "let's ask Dad for help and then 'bam' him" routine, but after a few ambushes, I got wise. When they wanted to quit, I was eventually smart enough to let them, and they would come back to it on their own.

My son got the benefit of the number his sisters had done on me, so I insisted that he take only two years of piano and two years of viola, and then I retired as my children's teacher before I could get hurt too badly. Mike went on to become a lawyer, among other things, doing some teaching at New York University Law School. Today he is my expert musicologist and bodyguard. Whenever I do some crazy thing that gets me into trouble, he drops whatever he is doing and rushes to pull me out of the ditch.

The joy I had listening to them advance through the years more than made up for the pain. To say that I'm proud of what my two girls have done with their musical careers is a giant understatement. Steffy was a member of the Cleveland Orchestra, was concertmaster of the San Antonio Symphony, and is presently a professor of violin and viola at the University of Nevada. Both girls have made more solo CDs than their dad, and this makes me just a little jealous. Seriously, one of my greatest thrills is appearing in concerts with them both. I'm just grateful that all three of my children love music, as I do.

If you are a musician yourself, and you teach your own children to play musical instruments, be warned: What goes around comes around. You are going to find that those once lovely youngsters can turn into monsters when they start working with you in your profession: "Dad, are you sure you want to play the B flat so low?" or "Dad, are you convinced that you are the only one who should make a retard before the coda—why don't you join the rest of us?" Or the direct approach from my other daughter, which is just as tough to take: "Dad, you are flat on the B flat and slowing down before the coda."

I hope no one pays attention to my girls. They are just having their revenge for all the annoying remarks I made to them when they were growing up. I never play flat and I never drag. So, there!

CHAPTER

43

PERKS

Symphony musicians often get some nice perks, at least in the Saint Louis Symphony we did. Half-price concert tickets, sometimes even free ones, special parking privileges, lovely hotel rooms, and ample spending money provided on tours to name a few. For me the greatest perk that came with being a symphony musician was the chance to be on the inside when the best conductors and soloists rolled up their sleeves and worked to put together a performance. Often the rehearsals were the most exciting times in a symphony musician's life. It was like watching a brain surgeon's most difficult operation or having a ringside seat when Michelangelo took his first whack at the marble hiding David.

How often I wished that I had a miniature video camera hidden in my cello scroll to record what went on in some of our more colorful sessions. Hilarity, tension, incredible displays of insight, quick-witted repartee, and every human emotion possible was displayed for all to see—all those who were on our Powell Hall rehearsal stage, that is.

I felt as if I was a member of a special club. Usually nobody else in the whole world, unless they, too, were in the club, would be allowed on our stage to share in our experiences. Neither money nor influence could open the doors to a rehearsal without an invitation. Even if you are a famous musician yourself, but not scheduled to perform with us, you ran the risk of being barred from our doors.

Once, while I was still with the BSO, a few of us from the Symphony tried to get into Carnegie Hall to hear a rehearsal of another orchestra that was performing the Brahms *Double Concerto for Violin and Cello in A minor*. Jascha Heifetz was appearing as both the conductor and violin soloist, with Gregor Piatigorsky as cello soloist. Any musician would have given his bow-arm to witness that rehearsal. We were salivating as we quietly entered the back of the hall. We assumed we would be welcome because, after all, we were in the same musicians' club, just a different chapter. Besides, our little group contained Joseph Silverstein, a famous violinist in his own right and the concertmaster of the BSO. Sticking close to Joey, we cautiously edged up to the stage from the rear of the darkened hall. We were a little uneasy in spite of all we had going for us, and we were hoping Jascha wouldn't notice our presence. Unfortunately he did, and after one look at us, it was clear that he didn't want anyone to hear him but his own musicians and those willing to pay $50 for a ticket.

"Out!" We got the message and awkwardly headed for the nearest exit.

Now, what we did next, you can always try too, but if you don't get away with it as we did, it might be embarrassing, so this is no endorsement. I knew of a very convoluted way that we could go into the building next door and then double back to enter the first balcony of the Carnegie, the hall from which we had just been booted. It was very dark, and some of us reasoned that if we crawled along the floor behind the seats and barely breathed, even Heifetz's super radar would not pick us up. It must have looked ridiculous—six grown men, up in a balcony, trying to sneak a peek at the forbidden rehearsal onstage—but we'd probably do it again if both artists were alive today. To see the greatest violinist of all time drill his orchestra over and over again in one of the more difficult passages of the concerto was to witness, for a moment, the creative drive of a legendary genius.

Usually I did not have to act as I did that afternoon, and that was what was great about my job. Instead of hiding on the floor one hundred sixty feet away from the action in some dark balcony in order to observe genius at work, I could sit in my comfortable chair six feet away from the conductor and hear his every word of wisdom. Even if you did manage to sneak your way into the back of the hall, I'm afraid you couldn't have had my vantage point. I was seeing the front of the conductor, and you could only see his rear.

CHAPTER

44

THAT CIGAR BOX WITH FOUR STRINGS

My instrument is so important to me that I often think of it as another member of my family. If it's not sounding good, I rush it off to the "doctor."

"My cello sounds like it has a cold," I'll tell Gene Bearden, who runs a wonderful instrument repair shop in northwestern St. Louis. When he tells me that he thinks he'll have to move the sound post just a little, it sends a shudder through me, and I feel as though I have just been told that one of my children is going to have a spinal tap. "Is it that serious?" I'll ask. The sound post is a four-inch piece of pinewood, shaped like a pencil, which is wedged inside the instrument under the right, if you are facing the cello, leg of the bridge. The slightest movement of this post will drastically change, for better or worse, the sound of the instrument.

"Well, we could try changing a string first. Let's see what your cello sounds like when I put on a new Larsen A string," Gene will answer.

We are constantly taking our "babies" in for check-ups. We're delighted when all that is wrong is a little opening in the side. This is something amazing about stringed instruments. They are designed to fall apart periodically. The glue that holds them together is very weak during periods of high humidity and very brittle during very dry weather. These are both times when there is great stress on the wood of these very valuable instruments. Instead of the wood cracking, which would be very expensive to repair, the instrument just falls apart at the point where the top or back meets the side. This is relatively easy to glue back together.

Besides being necessary tools to do our jobs, these instruments are extremely expensive, beautiful creations, which could easily be displayed in a museum if they were not needed onstage. My Carlo Tonini was made in 1703, is insured for an arm and a leg, and is probably one of the reasons I've had such a wonderful career. The soul of my playing is in its gorgeous sound. Even a clod can sound pretty good when he strokes its strings. These beautiful creations are so valuable to us that we never let them out of our sight. Well, rarely ever.

Now, if I tell you about the few times that I did forget to keep my eyes glued on my "baby," please don't go revising my psychological profile to include "forgetful" or "scatterbrained." We all slip-up occasionally, although most of us are afraid to admit it.

After flying to Japan on tour with our cellos buckled up in the front seats, most of my colleagues remembered to take them with them when they walked out the door of the plane. I think I was slightly preoccupied because I love Japan, and it wasn't until I reached customs that I noticed that I was alone. I had to figure out a way to gracefully go back and retrieve my cello without letting the rest of the orchestra, which was following me, know what a fool I'd been. By walking sideways and then backwards, I had almost pulled it off because people were not quite sure whether I was coming or going. Just as I casually reached the plane's main exit, I saw our personnel manager, Carl Schiebler, holding my cello as he stood blocking the doorway with a big grin on his face, which alerted the rest of the orchestra. Any stand-up comedian would have paid dearly for all the laughter I received from my colleagues. I never heard the end of it.

On another occasion, a friend of mine, who has a personality profile similar to mine, left his viola in his car in a parking garage. When he came back, there was no car. It appeared that his car had been stolen; thus he was minus a viola too, which conveniently got him out of one of our rehearsals. Not for long, though, since he soon discovered that he had gone to the wrong garage, and after redoing his navigation a bit, two of his most important worldly possessions were back in his hands.

Once, while on tour with the BSO in New York, I went to pay my hotel bill and check out. I put my two bags, which I brought down with me from the twelfth floor, on our tour bus outside the Wellington Hotel and then took the elevator up to get my cello, which I had wisely left locked in my room. The Joseph Guarnerius cello that I had at the time would be worth a fortune today. I was taking no chances with it. When I got back to my room and was just about to put the key in the door, I realized that it was already open and the maid was already starting to clean the room. As I walked in and commented on the hotel's efficiency, since I had just checked out, I looked around the room for my cello. It was gone!

I couldn't believe it. I asked the maid if she had seen a cello when she came into the room. I wasn't sure she that spoke English. With no luck there, I ran out of the room and down the hall, got the elevator to the lobby, and notified everyone—our management, the hotel management, the house detectives, my colleagues, and anyone else who would listen to me describe my horrendous loss. I hoped that they would muster enough people to guard all the exits to prevent the thief from escaping with the cello.

After alarming most of the occupants of the hotel and feeling pretty sure that every step was being taken to prevent the thief from leaving unobserved, I went up to my room to check again. There was always the possibility that the maid had put the cello in the closet, out of her way while she was cleaning. When I opened my door with the key, the maid was gone, the bed was unmade as I had left it, and my cello was sitting right in the middle of the room.

It was easy to figure out what had happened. Earlier I had stepped out of the elevator one floor too soon and had entered a corner room exactly like mine. The major difference was that it had a maid instead of a cello. Since the maid was already in the room, I didn't have to use my key, which would have tipped me off. That was easy to figure out. What was hard to figure out was how I was going to get out of this hotel, with my instrument, without being embarrassed in front of the whole BSO for not being able to find my own room, or worse, without being put in jail for trying to steal my own cello. Grabbing my instrument from the room, I quickly ran down the hall to the elevator, hoping to exit the hotel before the police showed up. When the elevator doors opened onto the lobby and fifty people rushed up to me, all I could think to say was, "Never mind."

CHAPTER

45

THE CAR CONSPIRACY

It was hard enough for me to always keep my eyes on my valuable means of livelihood, but when some outside force seemed bent on threatening its well-being, I really had my hands full. At times it seemed as if my cars were involved in a plot to "get" my cello. Preposterous, perhaps, but they may have had a motive. The great American love affair has been, for most of us, the affection we have for our cars. This has never been the case with me. I've loved only my instrument, and the automobile has simply been a means of transportation for my cello and me.

There's your motive. The cars were jealous! There was also the means and the opportunity for my cars to do great harm. As I said before, my theory is preposterous, but when I put several past incidents together, I saw a pattern. If nothing else, these incidents should have taught me not to leave my prized possession in a car for very long.

One close call was during a trip from St. Louis to a music camp I had created in 1994 in Steamboat Springs, Colorado. Every summer some of the staff and I usually formed a convoy of several vans and cars to ferry about twenty students across the Midwest to the mountains. That summer my car developed a problem, which made it conk out every five minutes when the temperature on the Kansas highway rose above 105 degrees. After several hours of frustration, I decided to let the rest of the convoy continue without me. There was hope that I would eventually be able to find some way to make my vehicle do better than one hundred-yards-an-hour and catch up with the rest of the convoy later in the evening at a motel in Colby, Colorado.

Sitting and roasting with my cello in the recalcitrant car by the side of the road, I contemplated my dilemma. There was no help in sight, no garages open on Sunday, and not much chance that I was ever going to get to my music camp in time to meet the incoming students. After waiting in vain for a police car or tow truck to notice me, I made one last effort to get the car started.

Turning the ignition key and pushing the gas pedal to the floor, the motor unexpectedly roared alive, and the van, my cello, and I started zooming down the highway. What I didn't understand at the time was that this car had the potential to destroy my cello and me. It had worked out something with its fuel pump in which only a constant acceleration of my speed would keep the motor going. My camp activity director, Meghan Buckley, who had also broken off from the convoy to accompany me, had been parked directly behind me. Just as I took off, she was calling the others at the camp on her cell phone to warn them that we weren't going to make it. Sensing that if I let up on the accelerator at all I would stall again, I gradually kept increasing my speed. Meghan couldn't figure out what I was doing and couldn't catch me either, because I was soon reaching speeds that should have been attracting an army of state police.

It was a challenge to stretch out the acceleration process, but I was getting so good with that gas pedal that it would take ten minutes to reach one hundred miles per hour. As soon as I let up on the gas even a little, the engine died and I was back by the side of the road. Sometimes I could get the car started again, racing ten miles at a time before Meghan reached me in her chase car. Once the car came to a complete stop, I could start up and begin the whole race-and-chase process all over again.

That car had put me in an uncomfortable position: Unless I was willing to live dangerously, my cello and I were not going to make Steamboat any time soon. The car knew me well and made every effort to tempt me to risk my cello and myself by driving like a maniac to reach my destination on time. Succumbing to the temptation, I made those short mad dashes across Kansas for two hours until I pulled off the road for some gas.

Here I was given some valuable information that enabled me to save my cello and myself from being destroyed in a highway accident by that wild driving. After I had complained about my car's behavior, a patron at the gas station explained that if I would wait about six hours for nightfall and a drop in the temperature, the car would stop its stalling. He told me that the overheated fuel pump would cool off by then and that we could drive like everyone else on the highway to reach our destination. He was right: After waiting for the sun to go down, we were able to drive all night, arriving safe, sound, and sleepy to greet the incoming students. But there is more.

Several years earlier while I was at our music camp in Massachusetts, another car of mine took a more direct approach. Leaving my little VW Bug parked on a flat driveway with my cello inside, I popped inside our main camp building to help my five-year-old daughter use the washroom. When I returned to where I had parked the car, it was gone. "Jack," I asked my friend, who was standing reading his mail where my car had been, "have you seen my car?" He told me that he saw it go around the house, but that he didn't notice who was driving it. No wonder. It had taken off on its own, moved over level ground, turned the corner of the building, and plunged down a hill one hundred yards into a huge grove of trees.

I ran around the corner of the house, hoping to catch the car before it got too far. I could see two tire tracks in the freshly cut field disappearing into the dense New England woods. Accompanied by about twenty campers, who had taken up the chase earlier, I raced into the forest darkness, fearing for my cello. The car's front end was wrapped around a tree, but the crash failed to harm my instrument, which was fairly well protected in its hard case in the back seat. It was barely out of tune. Wait, there is more, and the conspiracy theory gets even more convincing.

The most ingenious attempt by a car to harm my precious instrument happened on the Pennsylvania Turnpike in a freak spring snowstorm. The snow fell so suddenly and so thickly that I think it took everyone driving in the Pennsylvania hills by surprise. Our car began to lose power as the snow flew under the car and onto the ignition system, where it quickly melted from the heat of the engine. The resulting water then caused a short in the electrical wires leading to the motor, and our car gradually lost power.

We pulled over to the side of the road, and in that blinding snowstorm, put out the traditional, but useless, white handkerchief to alert the state police that we were in trouble. I told my wife, Peg, not to worry because the state police were constantly on the watch and would be by momentarily to rescue us. Nobody came, however, and eventually we began to get cold. I left my wife, a friend who was driving with us, and my precious cello in the car and began walking down the highway in that blizzard. I put out my thumb to see if I could avoid the long, cold walk to a gas station for help. The snow was falling faster, and I was surprised when, almost immediately, someone pulled over to pick me up. Now we had two cars parked by the side of the road in a blinding snowstorm with their parking lights on. This is what caused the ensuing chaos and the most dangerous threat to my cello imaginable.

Another car approached us. The driver became confused by our lights in the blinding snow, thought they must be off the road, and turned to join us on the shoulder of the highway. The car behind him smashed into his car. Many more cars were soon smashing into each other and narrowly missing my wife, friend, and cello, who were all still sitting in our vehicle by the side of the road. I ran back to get everyone, especially my cello, out of the car and out of the line of fire. With my wife holding my cello, my friend and I pushed her up an embankment to safety.

The scene was terrible, and there seemed to be no end to the crashes, as more and more cars piled up and into each other, always just missing our car. Running down the highway, I kept waving my hands, trying to warn the drivers to slow down before they, too, joined that great junkyard in back of me. This probably helped some cars avoid disaster, but every so often, a driver would think that he could make it through, and a few seconds after his car disappeared into a cloud of snow, I would hear a crash and a tinkle of broken glass. Drivers finally began to heed my warning, and my work was done. My wife came running after me and begged me to go back and warm myself in the car out of the wind and snow. It was now safe to bring the cello in from the storm too, because there were perhaps twenty to thirty cars, all with interlocked bumpers, forming a barrier between the oncoming traffic and our car.

It was an awful sight to behold, with cars in ditches and wedged together in such a manner that it would probably take half a day for the state police and the tow trucks, if they ever showed up, to clear the turnpike for through traffic. But with all the wrecks strewn behind us, making the highway look very much like those roads in Kuwait after the First Gulf War, there were very few banged up cars in front of us. Our way was clear.

"Wouldn't it be funny," I thought, "if the engine would start up now, and we could pull away from what we, in a way, have created?" A turn of the key enabled us to do just that. The water on the ignition, unbeknownst to us, had turned to ice. The engine, for a few minutes, was not being shorted or deprived of its all-important electrical charges. We sheepishly pulled back onto the highway, leaving thirty wrecked vehicles to take care of themselves, and slowly headed to the nearest gas station. We arrived just as our motor shorted out again. After we had some silicone sprayed on our ignition wires to prevent future engine trouble, I mentioned to the garage attendant that he might want to notify the state police about what I thought looked like a little accident back down the road a bit. It was the least I could do.

No, my cello was not damaged. Forget about those cars back down the road. Just tell me what you think of my theory.

46

AND TYLER, TOO

As conductors have changed from the aloof tyrants of sixty and seventy years ago to become the more human, but no less brilliant, leaders of today, so have guest soloists made a change more in keeping with the times. Often their appearances with us almost took on the look of a class reunion. Many of these artists enjoyed visiting with their school buddies who now played with us in the Symphony. Others, if they didn't know us before, got to know us after playing with us. They may have gone out after a concert for a late snack to continue the friendship. They are not only great artists, but also very warm people. Many took great pains to show their appreciation to all of us for our collaboration with them.

Yo Yo Ma, Sylvia McNair, Emmanuel Axe, and Jose Louis Garcia were great examples of artists who would go out of their way to be friendly and warm to both the Symphony musicians and those people in the audience wishing to meet them. Yo Yo never failed to ask about my cellist daughter before he even played one note. For Yo Yo, being nice to people is as gratifying to him as playing the Dvořák *Cello Concerto* with us. Manny Axe is from the same mold and would drag me to the front of the stage to share the limelight with him after I had a cello solo in his performance of the Brahms *Second Piano Concerto*. Sylvia even took time out of her incredibly busy schedule to write a letter of thanks for a small part I had played in one of her vocal concerts. Jose has taken so many musicians in the orchestra out for dinner that I couldn't keep tab on, and he was always the one who picked it up. We loved all these artists and always looked forward to their joining us.

For me, though, the great American institution, pianist John Browning, may have been the guest artist whom I most liked to see gracing our stage. Of course, he was a magnificent pianist and just as warm as those previously mentioned, but he had something else going for him that the others did not. He had Tyler, his little dog, who accompanied him everywhere he went. Tyler was as friendly as his master was, but he was also a great listener and a great connoisseur of piano music.

Once during a rehearsal of the Brahms *First Piano Concerto*, Tyler sat very quietly at John's feet in his little carrier box until the final chord of the first movement. Then he gave a little bark, almost

251

as if he knew that his master was finished for the moment. We in the orchestra all laughed and then plunged into the second movement. Tyler gave his little bark after the conclusion of this movement too. We laughed again, but now a coffee break was called before going on to the last movement of the concerto. John let Tyler out of his box, and he bounded over the stage, happy to be free at last.

Commenting to John about how it almost seemed that Tyler understood the music like a human, he assured me that his little friend really did hear just as we do. He told me all kinds of stories that were truly amazing. I don't think I believed him until I saw what happened after the break. John let Tyler sit out of his box way in the back of the first violin section as we read through the last movement. He stayed there quietly until the last fifteen or twenty bars of the piece. At that point, Tyler obviously recognized the Brahms chord progressions that would indicate to an experienced musician that the end was near, and he began running through the orchestra to arrive in his master's lap just in time for the final chord, but not a second before. At that point I became a believer.

CHAPTER

47

IS THIS YOUR REAL JOB?

Usually I'm not good at guessing people's occupations by just looking them over once and listening to a few seemingly innocuous statements come out of their mouths, but several years ago I managed to do just that with a person I had met for only two minutes. When I saw through his cover, he was shocked because he didn't think that his real job could ever be detected by casual observation. It never had been before that day, and his life often depended on keeping his true occupation hidden. If it weren't for the fact that we all live in such a small world, I wouldn't have guessed his line of work either.

This stranger happened to notice my cello case sitting near me and asked if I played the cello. When I said that I did, he told me that his best friend was a cellist. When he told me his friend's name, I immediately said, "Then you are a secret agent for the FBI, right?"

How did I do it? Easy. Although there are probably more than one hundred thousand cellists in the country, his best friend just happened to be a former student of mine, who was an undercover agent in the FBI. I put two-and-two together.

You don't have to be as lucky as I was that day or even an FBI agent to guess what I do for a living. What I carry around with me everywhere I go should tell everyone exactly what I do. But in spite of this, there are two questions that I am often asked as a symphony musician that reveal what a misunderstood group of people we are. For years I couldn't walk into a subway or an elevator with my cello without someone asking, "Do you have a machine gun in there?" There is something special about a cello case that makes people ask or jump to the wrong conclusion.

Once when that former cello student of mine in the FBI was going to take a commercial flight, he had to show his legal concealed weapon to the pilot before the other passengers boarded. FBI agents were, I guess, some of the few people who were allowed to carry guns on a plane, but the pilot's jaw dropped when my former student showed up with his cello case, which did contain his cello, not his registered revolver, which was in his shoulder holster. The pilot just assumed that he was going to have to worry about having a machine-gun on board.

The other question that I am often asked is, "What do you really do for a living?" This hurts because people are serious when they ask, which means that a lot of my fellow citizens have no idea how much work goes into what I do. Though musicians may not be on the job more than twenty hours a week, what time we do spend on the stage is very intense and can be incredibly draining. We don't have time to sit back and contemplate, but we are constantly being asked to respond immediately to written commands on a printed page at a speed determined by our boss, who is using hand and arm signals.

This boss, the maestro, also monitors everything we do and is not shy about expressing his displeasure with our work in front of everyone. A lot of us try to avoid making the boss too unhappy, thus risking public humiliation or worse. Therefore, we do a lot of extra work at home before we ever get to the Beethoven symphony assembly line. It's easy for conscientious symphony musicians, who are honing their craft and attending the required rehearsals, to put in six to ten hours a day playing their instruments. Though our work can be inspiring and gratifying, it can also be extremely exhausting.

Now you know—playing in an orchestra is our real job. Sure, most of the time it's fun, but don't hold that against us because it is still hard work. It's a full-time job, and it's difficult sometimes to have time for anything else. But we do. In fact, we seem to find the time to do just about everything imaginable.

When you look at the Saint Louis Symphony, with its members all decked out in their finest black uniforms, playing their hearts out, it may be hard to imagine, but you are looking at something other than just a group of talented musicians. There are amongst us carpenters, electricians, house renovators, a dancer, a seamstress, a fine violin maker, the founder and president of a canned coffee drink company, a wilderness explorer and whitewater river guide, an artist's manager, a radio announcer and commentator, a serious farmer, composers, car mechanics, computer experts, an investment advisor, a chess champion, many successful entrepreneurs, two sailors, and probably a lot more with avocations that I don't know about. Except for one of those sailors, me, all of them might have been good enough to make a career of their second love, if they had chosen to leave the Symphony.

Besides musical knowledge, a symphony orchestra is a mine of worldly information, which the musicians pass back and forth to each other to enrich their lives. It's obvious that an orchestra is a wonderful place to pick up tips to help one be successful at various music-related careers such as conducting or composing. Many people are surprised, though, when I tell them that there is a ton of very useful nonmusical information available within its ranks. For example, much of the knowledge that I gained about both of my outdoor passions, skiing and sailing, was learned during the intermissions of rehearsals in the Boston Symphony. I later did my graduate work in sailing during the intermissions of the Saint Louis Symphony rehearsals, although I never received a degree.

My lack of credentials, however, hasn't stopped my enthusiasm for the sport, and I've taken family, friends, and any colleagues who were willing to risk their lives sailing with me, up and down both coasts whenever time permitted. We have even been able, on occasion, to combine music and boating.

Once Roger Kaza, the present principal horn in the Symphony, brought along his instrument for a two-week sail in the San Juan Islands off our Northwest coast. After a glorious day of breezing around the islands, we would pull up each evening in charming little anchorages surrounded by the lovely cliffs and hills of those islands. Roger would serenade all the other boats until dusk with Mozart's *Horn Concerto*. Soon other sailors would row over in their dinghies to meet the "local" musician. I was amazed at what some well-executed horn calls would draw to our boat. I was even more amazed when Roger stuck the bell of his horn into the sea and blew a call that attracted a large minke whale to within twenty feet of us as we sailed through Puget Sound.

Though my sailing skills never reached the level of my two more experienced teachers in the BSO and the SLSO, I learned enough in the Symphonies to be able to navigate successfully in some pretty tricky waters. A Florida Keys navigation official has even accorded me the respected title of "Skipper." While trying to pass under a drawbridge between two islands in the Keys, I accidentally struck it with the top of my mast. My passage under it was a little premature: It hadn't opened yet. A message immediately came over my ship's radio: "Will the skipper of *Sea Breeze,* who just struck my bridge, please pull over to the wharf immediately?" Just as Leonard had enjoyed that first time he was addressed as maestro by a member of the SLSO, I, too, enjoyed hearing myself called by an important title. I wanted to hear that "Skipper" part again, not the part about the ticket I was expecting for hitting Florida state property.

CHAPTER

48

HIGH ANXIETY

Once during a Saint Louis Symphony Orchestra
rehearsal, our outstanding principal horn
uncharacteristically cracked one note slightly in
the famous horn solo in the slow movement of
Tchaikovsky's *Fifth Symphony*. That was, of
course, no big deal, and I'd hate to tell you all the
notes I have missed over the years. For Roland
Pandolfi, it was less than his usual perfect
playing. It was also the beginning of a couple of
days of, well, I'm not sure what he'd call it, but I'd
call it "high anxiety," and no musician wants it
around.

During the first concert on Thursday, his solo was
going just beautifully when he may have cracked
that note again. I'm not sure if it was exactly the
same note because, when you are pulling for a
colleague who may have a challenge, you really
don't listen too carefully, you just do a little of
that old-fashioned praying. That one minor slip
did not mar the rest of the seventy notes in the

solo, which he played with his usual gorgeous tone, but knowing that Roland is as much of a perfectionist as the rest of us, he could not have been happy. During Friday's concert, he again started out great, but it still didn't seem like his usual perfect playing. Oh, boy! This was getting serious. At times like this, there is a little devil that sits on your shoulder and tries to bump the angels off. It is screaming in your ear, "This is a trend, buster. One slip yesterday, two today, and tomorrow I am really going to embarrass you in front of two thousand people and all those well-wishing colleagues. You will be sorry you ever took up that horn!"

When you are where Roland was, you really start to let the world know what you are made of, because without a truckload of courage and some good insight, you are cooked. No one knows what was going on in Roland's head those next twenty-four hours or how he was figuring things out. When I saw him before Saturday's concert in the dressing room, he couldn't see me, or anyone else, for that matter, because he was so focused on the task ahead of him. Most of us have been in the same place that he was at that moment. We all have our own ways of talking back to that little devil. They are quite personal, and no one is going to brag about how he does it. In fact, if you ask him, he will say, "How do I do what?" The joy one has while expressing this beautiful music and a compulsion to share it with others is probably part of everyone's defense against the devil's propaganda.

That night, Roland again started out his solo as beautifully as he had the previous two evenings. Keep in mind that, through all of this, that seventeen feet of rolled up copper tubing with a mouthpiece stuck on one end is just about the trickiest piece of plumbing anyone will ever try to get a sound out of, let alone control enough to make the noise emitted from the big end resemble anything anyone could recognize as a tone. There is not a hornist, dead or alive, who hasn't blown it every once in a while. You almost have to start blowing before everyone else saws or bangs away on their instruments if you are going to get your contribution there on time. The conductor bows only to hornists and lets them say anything they want to during rehearsal. The conductor, along with the rest of the orchestra, is just happy that it is the fellow way in the back who must endure the hazards of playing the horn, not him. The conductor usually asks a French horn player; he does not tell him.

Halfway into the solo, Roland was nailing everything, and I began to realize that he had a chance for a perfect evening. This can be one of the toughest times in the whole experience as the little devil tries to get you to let up when you see the end in sight. Roland, however, must have seen nothing but the music, the conductor, and a chance to share his music with the audience. He soared through the last forty notes, taking a little time here and there to make Tchaikovsky's music even more effective. Such free playing is not easy, and many would not dare this kind of risk, especially after the little devil's warnings. At the conclusion of the performance, our conductor asked Roland, with a little sign language, if he could give him a special solo bow. The previous evening Roland had warned our maestro not to try. Roland consented and he smiled, but you could see that he wasn't letting up on his concentration yet, because tomorrow was another day and we had one more Tchaikovsky to play.

On Sunday Roland's solo was even better, if that was possible, and after his last bow, I thought I saw his shoulders finally relax a little. The expression on his face when I saw him in the men's locker room was that of a man who had been away on a long, hard journey and was glad to be back. We were happy to have Roland with us again; most of us were also glad that we don't play the French horn.

Oh, by the way, here is what the critic from *The New York Times* said when we played this symphony in Carnegie Hall: ". . . and particularly fine work was done by the horn section. . . . The Principal, Roland Pandolfi, should congratulate himself on a night of excellent work in which the great solo of the Tchaikovsky slow movement was only the icing on the cake."

I wouldn't mind having a review like this.

CHAPTER

49

IN THE LINE OF DUTY

In the spring of 1986 I looked at my cello section and was saddened to see that six of our twelve members were out with injuries, most of which had been received in the line of duty. The saddest part of this was that I was one of them. You normally don't think of playing in an orchestra as being a dangerous occupation. It shouldn't be, unless you get your stand-partner so peeved that he crushes his instrument over your head in frustration.

Unfortunately, from time to time, we do get hurt doing what we're paid to do and love so much. The situation that I just described is rare, and all but two of us were back soon. Sadly I was one of the two.

My problem started when I was touring in Japan in 1985 with the SLSO, and I was playing on my daughter's cello instead of my own. Sara, who had just won the bronze medal in the prestigious Tchaikovsky competition in Moscow, had been using my beautiful Tononi because it improved her chances at the competition by showing what a gorgeous tone she could produce. Contestants in major competitions often borrow the finest instruments that they can get their hands on. All the Russian cellists, against whom Sara was competing, were loaned great instruments by the state. Though Sara's own cello was weaker in sound production than mine, it was still a lovely instrument, fun to play, and some extra pressure from my bow arm seemed to make it speak out better. After a while though, I noticed a little pain creeping into my right arm during concerts.

At first I thought nothing of it. Realizing that I had been pressing very hard with my bow to make Sara's cello sound as good and as powerful as my own instrument, I started to ease up on the strings and bear down only in a few crucial spots that needed the extra effort. In spite of this, the pain increased. By the time I was back in the States, I was wincing on almost every bow stroke. I didn't want to let people know about my problem, because I didn't want anyone telling me to stay home. My attendance record up to then, not counting a few late arrivals caused by reading our symphony schedule incorrectly, was good, and my pride would not let me quit. But after a very vigorous Schumann *Third Symphony,* which we played just before Christmas vacation, I had had it, and I felt that it would be irresponsible for me not to let the management know that I was in trouble.

For the better part of a year, I had to stay home. At the Symphony's request, I visited eleven of the best doctors and therapists in the country, including the doctor for the St. Louis Cardinals baseball team and the physical therapist for the St. Louis Blues hockey team. I was videotaped playing the cello, x-rayed, stuck with needles, given physical therapy, and given slings for my arm to rest in. Nothing really helped. Eventually the whole right side of my body was in agony, and all I could do was sit in the living room and mope. Attending rehearsals and watching my friends in the Symphony playing away on the stage of Powell Hall only made me feel worse. I had to do something else to fill up my life, or I would go crazy. Since Red Fox Music Camp had closed in 1979, seven years earlier after my mother died, I thought it was the right time to start another one, and I knew that running a camp would certainly fill up my days.

For about five summers after I had sold Red Fox, I had played first cello in the Grand Teton Music Festival Orchestra in Jackson Hole, Wyoming, under the direction of Ling Tung, who had been a buddy of mine in the Seventh Army Symphony. After playing for two months in the shadow of those magnificent peaks, I fell in love with the West and its beautiful mountains. It was

266

appropriate, then, that I should name my new camp Strings in the Mountains.

The last summer before my injury, I had taken ten cello students with me to the Teton Festival, where I juggled playing in the Festival Orchestra, giving students cello lessons, taking kids on canoe trips, and going on hikes high up into the mountains. That time in the Rockies had been great fun.

When I faced the next summer, with no prospect of getting back in the Symphony soon, I decided to make my little seminar into a larger camp. This time I added the violins, violas, and basses. I took my camp to the lovely town of Steamboat Springs, Colorado, where, up on the slope of Mt. Werner, I had found a wonderful condo complex called Storm Meadows, in which to house my students.

While I ran the camp with an almost useless right arm that first summer, I began looking for a place to start a small chamber music festival for the next year. I decided on an old athletic club, which was also perched up high on the side of the mountain, right next to our little school. The owners of the club, John and Betse Grassby, liked my idea of using their huge deck, with its glorious views of the surrounding mountains and the Yampa Valley, as an outdoor concert hall. Thus began Strings in the Mountains.

Betse teamed up with me to plan our first season. She was a marvel at reaching everyone in town who would either come to the concerts or help us set them up. Her networking, along with the teachers from my music camp, including my daughter Sara, who all played for free, helped us get off to a good start. It was a great success, and we began to grow so fast that we almost couldn't believe what was happening.

The following summer, we added another wonder woman by the name of Kay Clagett, who took over our fund-raising. We began to grow even more. Kay would successfully raise the funds to meet the $500,000 budget necessary to present our ambitious programs. We won some prestigious prize for being the most exciting new festival in Colorado, which wasn't bad in a state that has more music festivals, including the world-famous Aspen Music Festival, than any other state in the Union. We also made it onto a television program, *CBS News Sunday Morning* with Charles Kurault.

We didn't stop at chamber music. After several years we added pop, jazz, and gypsy. We also added some little theater, inviting Loretta Swit, Tony Francisco, and Kevin McCarthy to do one- and two-man shows. As I mentioned before, Leonard Slatkin and his wife, Linda, came out to perform for us. It is interesting to note that all of this occurred because of my arm injury. About seven years after I had injured my arm, and just when I thought that my great vision was complete, cracks began to appear. A good friend once said to me, "John, you tend to push people a little too much." While we were running a school for seventy students, we were also giving festival performances every night of the week and twice on Sunday. The hotels liked this crazy schedule, but not everyone in the music festival administration was thrilled about my pace. No one else but me seemed to want the moon. I was just barely winning my points in board meetings.

Seeing the handwriting on the wall and not yet having conquered a little, or maybe a tinge, of self-righteousness, I reluctantly resigned as music director of Strings in the Mountains and eventually started a new summer music school called Mountain Team Concepts. I later passed the school on to my friend Ernest Richardson. It is now called Rocky Mountain Conservatory. My departure was very sad for me because I thought that the vision was not yet complete. Perhaps I was wrong, because those who stayed on have continued to make Strings in the Mountains one of the best music festivals in the country. They probably restored a little sanity to the project by eventually cutting weekly events from eight to five and closing the school. Then they sent—I'm sure unintentionally— a message that I'm afraid I still don't get: They hired three people to replace me. Maybe it wasn't only the other people who I was pushing too hard. Am I a workaholic? Of course not!

CHAPTER

50

SOME GOOD ADVICE

After the first season with my new camp in Steamboat Springs, I returned to St. Louis, but not to the Symphony. I still hadn't seen any improvement in my injured wing, despite all the rest I had given it from the cello during the summer months. In 1986 some of us around the country were beginning to learn some things about musicians' playing injuries that were not yet commonly known. Often these injuries were very puzzling to doctors because it was hard to see exactly what was wrong. How to cure them was even harder. They weren't anything like baseball or hockey injuries. The most common diagnosis was "over-use syndrome," but that concept was hard for us to accept because it made you think, "Let's see, just how many down-bows do I have left in me today?" This just didn't seem to make sense. As my friends and I conferred over the phone, certain facts were becoming more and more evident.

271

First, rest alone never seemed to help much, and most of us found that we had to keep the injured limb or neck moving freely, not favor it or put it in a sling.

Second, the night before making the effort to return to work was often the most painful, as fear would try to contract every muscle that one allowed oneself to even think about.

Third, most of us had to "play through" our injuries. By that, I don't mean that just sat there in the orchestra mindlessly sawing away, ignoring the ripping and tearing that seemed to be occurring in our damaged limbs, and hoping that the injuries would just go away. We learned that we had to calmly search for what we were doing wrong and know that we had an unlimited number of down bows and up bows available for use each day, as long as our arms were doing them corrcctly. We often had to leave our colleagues in order to work it out at home or on top of a mountain.

Severe pains in my neck, right shoulder, and almost every finger of my right hand had to be worked out on the job. Sometimes it is hard to find the source of the problem, because it could be some new little thing that you are doing with your hand to improve your sound, which you discovered a week earlier, and the effects of this change in your playing are just starting to show up in that day's rehearsal. Then you have to go back and do some detective work to find the wrong motion or position.

Keep in mind that we can often be at our instruments for ten hours a day. This means that we have to bow correctly at that moment, or we may suffer later. Maybe the professional aspects of our work show why they pay us, like doctors, lawyers, and ballplayers, so much. I'm kidding, of course. It's a fact that there may be only one opening for a flutist in a major city's professional orchestra every ten or fifteen years, while that same large city's many law firms will take in hundreds of new associates between them every year. They should pay us more, or at least pay the flutist more.

Occasionally some of us simply cannot figure out what we are doing wrong. That was true in my case. I had consulted with almost a dozen physical therapists, including sport therapists, as well as doctors, in three cities over a period of a year. Videos didn't show anything. My friends couldn't see the problem; nor could I, after I played in front of a mirror for months. At times like that, there might have been only one solution, and that was to let go.

I decided to call a Christian Science practitioner to get rid of the pain. I was struggling hard for a solution. This struggle, in fact, blocked inspiration. For me, inspiration usually comes from God. The practitioner prayed for me, and the resulting inspiration rescued me. One day, when I wasn't trying so hard, it came to me: "You've got long arms; let's try something different. You have held the bow with your right hand, as ninety-five percent of all cellists do, for almost forty years. Why not put your right pinkie on top of the stick, more like a violinist holds his bow?"

With nothing to lose at this point, I tried applying what my inspiration seemed to be advising. This slight shift in my grip on the bow seemed to change the angle of my right elbow just enough, so that when I drew the bow, my arm was moving in a manner different from what I had noticed before. As I had tried many different positions in the past year with no success, I wasn't sure that anything was going to be better this time. It was tricky to tell if this was working because it always takes time to test the effect of a new idea.

Something told me, probably my intuition, to stick with it this time and be patient. I did, and the pain didn't increase. After a week or two of using the new grip, I noticed that a definite decrease in discomfort was occurring. Bingo! My intuition had provided good advice. I would need no Purple Heart, and I was back in the trenches within a couple of months. I have enjoyed playing music pain-free ever since.

CHAPTER

51

THE GREAT DEPRESSION

Depressions are depressing to talk about, so I won't go on long about the doozy that I had. But I did learn some valuable lessons from it that might be worth mentioning. Because of its severity, I was forced to develop a great "Antidepression Kit" that they should pass out in all psychiatrists' offices. I am sure that the kit would save people a lot of money and time.

When my depression hit, my world went from beautiful Technicolor to old-fashioned, dismal black and white. I was usually an upbeat person, but overnight I became mostly downbeat. In this case, these were not musical terms. Getting rid of myself was not an option, but it was so bad that if I had been told that I had gotten onto the Mafia's hit list, I think that my day would have been made.

Who knows why it happened. Probably something to do with some guilt that I wasn't dealing with properly. One of my symptoms was that I couldn't answer a question without examining my answer over and over again, to be sure that it was the most absolutely honest and up-to-date reply that I could come up with. People were getting afraid to even ask me about the weather, fearing that the seasons would change before I ever finished my response. As a wise friend described it, I was getting a bit too zealous about being truthful. All this didn't concern me as much as how I was going to get rid of the gloom.

This black cloud appeared in the early 1970s. I was in St. Louis, in my early forties, and did not have my mother or my wonderful aunts around to fix it. Whenever a problem like this came up, they would say, "Don't worry, it will go away," and it always did. Now I was a big boy and had to dig into my troubled childhood if I ever wanted to smile again. Well, I tried the digging routine for five weeks, but I felt as if I were back in Massachusetts, emptying that infamous out-house in the rain again. So, without Mom and my aunts around, and not being into pills, I went to talk to—who else?—our beloved Henry Loew, who was our personnel manager as well as the Symphony's principal bass.

Henry always had time to talk to everyone. He came up with the first item in my Antidepression Kit: a book on walking. "Walk," he said. "Walk until your legs fall off." And I did.

Next, my wife, Peg, told me something like, "You know, all this whining about how depressed you are isn't helping the family. It's not easy to take.

Try not pouring it out on us twenty-four hours a day and instead start dealing with it yourself." That was good advice, for which I am eternally grateful. I ran out and got the second item, a smile. You can always cut out a nice paper one and paste it on your lips until you can get your face to remember exactly how to create a real one.

Wearing this fake smile, I did a lot of walking and pretending that I was happy. People started looking at me and commenting, "Well, I see John is over his stupid depression. What did he have to be so depressed about anyway?" It was funny, but all this walking and acting was starting to help. While keeping a daily picture diary, in which I made a round circle for a face and put in a mouth that indicated how I felt that day, I could see a trend occurring. Every so often a face would almost have a little upward curve at each end. That gave me hope.

Now, the last item you need for your Antidepression Kit is a cello. You don't need an expensive one like my Tononi. Gene Bearden's Violin Shop in St. Louis has a nice assortment of antidepression cellos and violins that will fit anyone's budget. Playing a musical instrument does wonders for depression. If you can ever find a way to do all three of these things at the same time, I'm sure that you'll come out of it more quickly than I did. So, equipped with my Antidepression Kit, I licked that black cloud in six months. Nothing bothers me now. Even if I lose $10,000 in the stock market, I get over it right away, or at least in six months.

CHAPTER

52

MARILYN

The definition of the word "conscientious" in my dictionary would have been our Marilyn Beabout. This devoted lady and fine cellist has probably left more tangible evidence of her thirty-seven years with the Saint Louis Symphony than anyone I can think of. Marilyn was so dedicated that a former principal cellist of the Saint Louis Symphony, whom I replaced, told me in a telephone conversation before I arrived, "Marilyn Beabout will be the most helpful person that you will ever have in your section."

Marilyn's specialty was getting all the pencil marks that would be helpful in performing the music correctly into her part, and into your part, and into everyone else's part that she could momentarily steal when his back was turned. Ninety-nine percent of the time this was extremely helpful, and ninety-nine percent of the time performances were better because of her "caring kleptomania." But Marilyn was human, just like the rest of us; she slipped up on one or two occasions.

Once, after taking all our cello parts out overnight and spending hours synchronizing every little mark that could guide us to more easily play our music the next day, she must have taken a short, well-deserved cat nap between 5:00 and 6:00 A.M. The alarm clock doesn't always wake someone who works this hard and long, so it was no surprise that the orchestra started the rehearsal at 10:00 A.M. without cellos, because our music was still with Marilyn, who was asleep at her worktable. The management was not too happy about this, but frankly, I felt that it was worth the risk to let Marilyn continue doing all this helpful extra work for us, as she had been doing for so many years.

Marilyn had so many marks, signs, and outright directions written all over my music that I didn't even have to think while I was reading my part. I truly appreciated it. Many a conductor thought that I was such a sensitive cellist, when in fact I was just following Marilyn's instructions. She had a piece of pencil lead taped to the tip of her bow and an eraser on the screw of her frog, the other end of a bow. She could play and mark her music almost at the same time by using her bow as a giant pencil. When she had a beat or two rest, Marilyn could put the point of her bow on the page that she was reading from and scribble in the margins. Since she couldn't take too much time to mark something while we were all supposed to be playing, she developed a special, easy-to-apply hieroglyphics system, which to this day no one else can read.

Marilyn also kept small binoculars in her purse so that she could see the smallest mark that I might put on my music, all the way from the back of the cello section. Her lunches, which also came out of that practical purse of hers, were eaten during breaks on the stage so that she could add more markings and never interrupt her work. I don't think that I ever saw her eating in the musicians' lounge with the rest of the orchestra.

On her rotated days off, I would find her in full dress, marking our parts during the intermissions of an opera performance that she was not required to attend. She didn't have to be there, she didn't have to be in full dress, and she could have been out walking in Forest Park, as I would have been if I had had a day off. Now, I know you think I'm exaggerating, but ask anyone who knows her. She was proud of all that she did for us, as she should have been.

Once all her extra work almost got both of us in trouble. It was the only time I had enough presence of mind to ignore what she had so carefully written into the music. We were playing a Samuel Barber opera, which has solos for two cellos. My stand-partner and I had to play these solos one after the other, sort of answering each other. Marilyn, who had not played this work on the stand with me before, was replacing my regular assistant for just that evening's performance. Marilyn, being as thorough as she was, looked for every special mark she had put into her own part. She then transferred all those pencil markings from her part to mine. She must have transferred more than fifty marks, all correctly, except one.

Right above these important solos, which she was to share with me, she had written "in 6," when she should have written "in 3." Our solos came immediately after a page turn. We didn't have time to think too long about what was coming up next. When she turned the page, the solos were upon us. I had not even a second to read her incorrect penciled instructions.

My solo was first. I started playing the tune that should soon have been answered by Marilyn. She, however, still had two very long measures to go by her calculations, so she didn't even have her bow up yet, ready to play. Sensing her confusion, I jumped down a line on the page, after finishing my first melody, and played her solo. Then I jumped back up a line and played my second solo. She still didn't get the picture. It looked as though she was not going to join me anytime soon. So I kept jumping back and forth between her solos and mine until they were finished.

Through all this, Marilyn was still counting with her bow by her side, occasionally glancing at me with a puzzled look. The conductor never even noticed the one-man show going on below him. In fact, no one else in the orchestra knows that Marilyn had never played her solos because no one was watching us. Please don't let the secret out because I'm just grateful that I had the opportunity to repay Marilyn for all she did for me during those twenty-six years.

CHAPTER

53

MORE GOOD ADVICE

If you are not a conductor, you can skip this chapter. This is only for the eyes of those men and women who wave batons at large groups of musicians and like to be addressed as Maestro.

Maestros, are we alone? OK. Now, I've been watching you guys for fifty years, and I think I can tell you a thing or two about your jobs, and how you can do them better. No, I don't want to be a conductor myself, because I tried it once and I wasn't any good, but that doesn't stop me from putting my two cents in here.

Where do we start? Probably with the advice that Sir Thomas Beecham gave to young aspiring conductors: "Start beating when we begin, don't annoy us while we play, and stop when we stop."

This is good advice, but I'm sure that most of you can do more than this already. It is true, however, that I have worked with conductors who could never get started properly; with others who were particularly annoying during entire performances because they were preoccupied with preventing the musicians from doing musical things that were not their ideas; and with one who beat an extra measure after the orchestra had played the last chord. Sir Thomas Beecham had some good advice, so don't ignore it.

What I think is more important for you leaders to learn is that your demeanor can make or break you with an orchestra more than all the fancy beating or deep musical insight that you could ever pull out of your talent bag. Believe it or not, the musicians want to like and trust you and to play their hearts out for you, but if you don't indicate that you feel the same way about them and appreciate what they are doing, you will slowly lose them. It may take a year or so, but it can also happen very quickly. I've seen it happen in one rehearsal. Don't ask who it was.

Scowling, though not recommended, can occur, but it has to be balanced almost immediately with smiles, and tons of them. To me the hardest task you have, standing up on that podium in front of one hundred musicians, is to make everyone believe that you are personally feeling great, happy to be there with them, and sure that what you are about to rehearse will be a piece of cake for the musicians, because you have such confidence in them. You may be sick with the flu, suffering from the usual conductor's paranoia, and scared that the piece you are about to conduct is impossibly difficult, but keep it all to yourself. I have seen a music director warn an orchestra for weeks about how hard a piece is, and then have a self-fulfilling prophecy on his hands. It's wise, of course, when one of these monster works looms before you, to suggest to the musicians, in an offhand way, that they might want to look at the Bartok *Concerto for Orchestra*, but for heaven's sake, don't terrorize your musicians.

In other words, besides having to be a great musician, you also have to be an actor and follow Beecham's advice, whether or not you believe it. Nobody ever said it was going to be easy.

Recently I heard an outstanding conductor lament that he tended to say nothing if the music coming from the orchestra is magnificent and commented only when he thought he needed to correct something. That's a built-in problem with your job. I know that you are not getting paid to spend your time praising us, and in a way, your salary is based on how good you are at finding fault with us. I understand that, but here's where a smile, when we are magnificent, can do wonders. It's better than all the words of praise you could ever give us, though a spoken "that was beautiful" once in a while wouldn't hurt.

That's all the advice I have for you, Maestros. Start with us, stay out of our way, and end with us, but most important, be sure to smile the whole time. That way you'll always keep out of trouble, with us, at least.

CHAPTER

54

CONCERTMASTERS I HAVE KNOWN

The concertmaster is the violinist who sits directly to the left of the conductor and who gets to shake his hand before the music begins. I have known many concertmasters over the past fifty years. They are a special breed. I usually like them. Some of my best friends were concertmasters. Some of my worst enemies were too. Of course that's all in the past. Maybe they had good reason to be unhappy with me. I wasn't always as respectful to them as I should have been.

Now, in my mature years, I can see that it was a mistake on my part because, next to the conductor, the concertmaster position is the hardest job there is. How do I know? Well, for one, two concertmasters were more than just my friends, they were my family members: my second wife, Nina Bodnar, former concertmaster of the Saint Louis Symphony, and my oldest daughter, Stephanie Sant'Ambrogio, former concertmaster of the San Antonio Symphony. I'm close enough to them to know that it's not a position you take lightly.

It's not easy to get the job in the first place because almost every violinist in the world thinks that it's what he or she wants. The competition is keen. At one of the searches for a concertmaster for the Saint Louis Symphony, the orchestra invited a number of concertmasters from other orchestras around the nation to come and play for our audition committee on the stage of Powell Hall.

But we also accepted applications from other outstanding violinists, who had with fewer credentials. All the contestants, except for the specifically invited and nationally recognized concertmasters, were asked to play their auditions from behind a screen, which the stage hands had erected to hide the applicants. One candidate in particular was so impressive that the members of the audition committee were unanimous in their approval of what they had just heard. This violinist had played with such command and strength that I was suspicious that it might be one of the more experienced artists, who had mistakenly been included with the younger players. After we had taken our secret votes on this brilliant player and were indulging in a ten-minute coffee break, the assistant personnel manager appeared from behind the screen. I shouted to him, "Hey Joe, that last guy was incredible!"

"That last guy was a gal!" he answered.

After months of more auditions, that gal, Nina Bodnar, became the concertmaster of the Saint Louis Symphony. Four years later she also became my second wife.

Getting the job isn't easy, but keeping it is no lark either. To survive as a concertmaster of a major orchestra one has to be a superb violinist, a deep musician, have great interpersonal skills or thick skin or both, and know how to walk a tightrope. It has been said that the concertmaster often serves as the conductor's ambassador to the players as well as the players' strong voice to the conductor. In other words, a concertmaster had better know how to walk a tightrope.

During my tenure with two symphony orchestras, I played under six different concertmasters, and it had been fascinating to watch each of them as he made his way across our Niagara Falls on that high wire. Some slipped off. Usually there was a net underneath, like another good job, which caught him just before he hit the rocks. After getting over the unpleasant plunge, he went on to another orchestra. There he climbed up again on that wire and made it across the second time. Those who made it the first time are the ones who never cease to amaze me.

The responsibilities of the concertmaster are endless if he takes the position seriously; any other way will only get him fired. To start with, the concertmaster must play the violin better than anyone else within earshot, probably as well as a soloist who might appear with the orchestra. Also, a concertmaster will usually appear as a soloist with his own orchestra at least once a year. Besides all the challenging violin solos from the orchestral literature that will come his way weekly, he will constantly be asked by the conductor, during rehearsals, to stand up in front of his colleagues and demonstrate just how a particular passage in the music should be played.

This means that he has to know everything cold before the orchestra does its first read-through and not be too hung up on being forced to show off at a moment's notice. Doing all this should not tax the concertmaster too much or he will wear out fast. Most concertmasters with long tenures are usually calm people who don't make a big deal about their jobs, which, however, is a big deal.

There is simply no way you can hide as a concertmaster. The maestro is so close to and focused in on that first chair that he can tell whether or not the concertmaster's notes are perfectly in tune, if they're exactly with him, and if they are of the proper dynamic. He can even pass judgment on the quality of his tone, color, vibrato, and cologne. It's really a hot seat.

Now, while all this attention is directed his way, the concertmaster must stay relaxed, so as not to sustain an injury, and then confidently lead the violin section and sometimes the whole orchestra throughout every performance, always being the definitive interpreter of the conductor's beat, no matter how puzzling it may get. It's been said that the tip of the concertmaster's bow "is often the beacon other players need in complex music or in situations where they can't hear each other onstage."

That briefly sums up the concertmaster's duties onstage. That may usually be the easiest part of his assignment. There is much more. The concertmaster, before the first rehearsal, must put hundreds of pencil marks, called bowings, in the first stand violin music, which will eventually enable the entire string section to phrase/breathe together. Putting those pencil lines on the page, which indicate the number of notes that a string player should play on each swipe of his bow, can take hours to do each week. Again, this is the easy part. Not so easy is ignoring the critical comments from your colleagues, and sometimes from the conductor, if the bowings aren't to their liking. Here is where that thick skin comes in handy. Or you could try intimidation.

Some concertmasters use this weapon very effectively to quell dissent from within the ranks. Those who wield this weapon with arrogance, however, usually suffer themselves, in the end, from a groundswell of resentment from everyone else around them. Others, like Joey Silverstein, the brilliant former concertmaster of the Boston Symphony and a man who is often called the dean of concertmasters, could look at you with a benign expression on his face, not even raise a corner of one of his beautiful bushy eyebrows, speak to you in a kind, fatherly fashion, and still make you feel as if you were only two feet tall.

How? I neglected to mention that, as he was talking to you, he was also impeccably playing the Stravinsky *Violin Concerto,* gripping both his bow and a lighted cigarette with the fingers of his right hand. At the same time, he was seated at the card table backstage, playing his cards with his left hand whenever he could free it up during an open string passage. I also forgot to tell you that, while all this was going on, I wasn't the only person to whom he was talking. One of the other conversations was with someone who was interested in hearing about Joey's recent performance with Isaac Stern. Now tell me, honestly, would you question the bowings of somebody like that?

Another responsibility, no less important than all of the above, is chairing the violin audition committee. Though the concertmaster in our orchestra had just one vote like everyone else at auditions, his input was vital, because his colleagues appreciated any guidance that he could give in setting a standard that the committee could refer to during the auditions. After all, if everyone agrees that the concertmaster knows what he's doing on the stage, then maybe we should know what qualities he would like to see in the musicians around him. I have witnessed occasions in the past, however, when differing opinions between the concertmaster and a good portion of the committee made it necessary for the concertmaster to have exceptional interpersonal skills in order to resolve the dispute. Not every concertmaster had them, and this would often ignite some interesting fireworks.

Most concertmasters soon find that they have to develop some good social skills outside the concert hall as well. The concertmaster often puts in as many hours offstage in committee rooms as he does onstage in his concertmaster seat. It may not be in his official job description, but the concertmaster is one of the most important ambassadors that the symphony has. Graciousness is a must.

Still, the hardest part of the job is walking that tightrope. To be successful, it's a given that the concertmaster has to have all the aforementioned qualities. If the concertmaster wants to avoid either ulcers or the ax, he has to learn to keep his balance up there on the high wire.

Many conductors expect concertmasters to be on "their side." That can immediately make for trouble. The concertmaster should stay on the good side of his conductor if he plans to stay awhile, but the concertmaster does live in the land of the players, not in the rarefied air of the podium. If the concertmaster sides too strongly with either party, he can start to lose that all-important equilibrium. I've seen a concertmaster lean first in one direction, ally with the conductor against a player being considered for dismissal, quickly switch sides, ally with his colleagues supporting the endangered player, and then promptly get fired. I've seen another concertmaster try the same thing, only this time reversing the order of his leaning, with the same unpleasant results. Neither way works.

A concertmaster must stay right in the middle of that wire. He must be the best diplomat in the city. David Halen, the present concertmaster of the Saint Louis Symphony, probably is. David is a superb musician with impressive violin skills, but he did not go to one of the larger, more famous music conservatories such as Julliard, Curtis, or Indiana University.

Katie Mattis, the Symphony's associate principal violist, once said to me, after a Saint Louis Symphony quartet rehearsal of the Ravel *String*

Quartet, "Isn't it wonderful how pleasant and relaxed our practice was? It must be David." It was. Also, the tone he set at that practice was a far cry from some of the wars that posed as quartet rehearsals that I've attended in the past. So, how did David get so good at all this? I have a theory.

Though he got terrific musical instruction, he was also surrounded by many students who were getting a broad liberal arts education, not just focusing on the field of music. David started his orchestral career in the first violin section of the Houston Symphony, not as a concertmaster. There you have it. This common-man feeling that David gives off and his broad-based background prepared him to be such a great diplomat. In fact, his background is quite similar to mine. Now I want to know where I went wrong.

All the concertmasters with whom I have played over the years have had qualities besides their musical talents that have contributed to my education and pleasure. Richard Burgin, one of the legendary concertmasters of the BSO, taught me humility and compassion. Joey Silverstein, besides personally giving my students and me tons of his valuable free time, set standards for me that are still a challenge. Max Rabinovitsj, the concertmaster who was in the Saint Louis Symphony when I first arrived fifty years ago, showed me an energy and enthusiasm that was contagious. This enthusiasm was responsible for bringing many fine players to the Symphony. Jacques Israelivitch was an expert on performance practices in music. He brought a wealth of valuable musical information from his years of experience in the Chicago Symphony. David Halen brings everything and himself, and just the latter is enough. Then there was my favorite, my former wife, Nina Bodnar. OK, maybe I am a little biased.

Nina is an incredible violinist. Once, after a concert the Symphony played in Carnegie Hall, Isaac Stern rushed backstage to comment on how amazingly beautiful the solos were that he had just heard. It was Nina who played them. Many very talented violinists followed her to the Saint Louis Symphony when she took the position in 1991, just to be around her artistry.

What impresses me most about Nina is that she ultimately went with her heart, not a desire for fame. During the third of her five years with the Symphony, she developed a violinist's injury that only a violinist could understand. She had to take a leave, just as I had twenty years earlier. I wouldn't stop bugging her to go back, no matter what. Fortunately she ignored me. Today she is teaching and inspiring young musicians in Santa Barbara, California. She is happier than she has ever been. Recently I was playing in an orchestra filled with students of hers. We were performing for a packed house. The smiles on the students' faces as well as those of the audience members matched hers, as she observed her "children" soaring.

OK, maybe there is more to life than being a concertmaster.

CHAPTER
55

THOSE NEWCOMERS

There were a lot of things in my life that came together to help plunk me down in the middle of this world of professional symphonic music. It wasn't just the U.S. Army or our Red Fox music camp that prepared me for my career. Having two good musicians for parents didn't hurt either. I think having the chance to hear them play day in and day out was more important than whatever genes they might have shared with me. Although I got a late start on the cello at fifteen, my mother wouldn't stop telling me, "You can do it! You can do it!"

My father, on the other hand, was always trying to do it, and just about anything else he could think of. His willingness to investigate everything that took his fancy made him a good role model in the explorer's department. Another help along the way was having a best friend and college roommate, Jack Ervin, who was also a fine musician and pianist. He would, for example, stay up until four in the morning listening to symphony recordings because he was as crazy about classical music as I was. Friends! Thank God mine were good.

I can't forget those wonderful aunts and uncles, who used to make a fuss over my music whenever I visited them, which was often. Later they made the same fuss over my children's performances. I also can't forget those enthusiastic cello teachers, who passed on their artistry to me, sometimes free, and were usually forgiving of my momentary dense periods.

Who knows, maybe the most important help that I received was from that all-important truck driver who picked me up when I was hitchhiking from college to that lesson with Paul Olefsky in Philadelphia. Paul, in turn, was the teacher who got me into Tanglewood's Berkshire Music School, where I was lucky enough to win the Piatigorsky Prize, which enabled me to study with Leonard Rose, which in turn helped get me into the Seventh Army Symphony, which helped prepare me for . . . There were too many good things for me to list that were out of my control that came together to put me on center stage. For instance, there was family.

Each member of my family helped me in different ways. Each contributed to my having a rich and joyful life, but I didn't see this while I was growing up. In fact, I felt something crazy was going on, and I didn't understand how their different approaches actually worked together to help me.

For example, my father and mother gave me a course called Life 101. It would start with my father saying, "John, you are mediocre." He was reading from the old-time teaching technique book. My mother would then take me aside and say, "That's not true." Years later, when I got out into the real world, the real world said, "John, you are mediocre," which it loves to do to all of us. I would remember what I had learned from that Life 101 course. Then I would ignore the first claim, and embrace the second and keep going. Now, even though my father seemed a little insensitive to my too-sensitive nature, he alone was the expert who could tell me with whom I should study cello. While part of his parental assignment was to put me in my place, he was also the one who was responsible for sending me to some of the best teachers in the country.

My Italian grandparents, uncles, aunts, and cousins were the ones who really saved me. When the Life 101 course got too tough to handle, I, at eight years of age, would walk five miles to Grandma's house to get a break. That's where my two favorite aunts, Gilda and Margaret, lived. They treated me as if I was normal. The time spent in Little Italy in Bloomfield, New Jersey, was my delicious recess from the Life 101 class in my home.

Then there was my brilliant Uncle Henry. He saved me many times from the over-emphasis on "you are mediocre" in my life classes. When things were getting a little too rough, he would often diplomatically offer a gentle suggestion to a professor or two. Once, in 1956, when I was attending the Life 102 class, which was held at Ft. Dix, New Jersey—also called Army Basic Training—he heard that some of my buddies and I were being badly treated by some sergeants.

I guess this information was passed on to him by my parents after they received my whining phone calls. It didn't take Uncle Henry two seconds to figure out how to instruct my instructors. He put on his U.S. Army Reserves major's uniform, got in his car, and drove several hundred miles to visit me at my barracks. Miraculously, after he had told the sergeants, "I'd like to visit my nephew, John Sant'Ambrogio," things improved markedly. Thank God for family.

That's also what makes an orchestra, like the Saint Louis Symphony, so great: a million little things that happened to each of one hundred people from all over the country (and the rest of the world, including China, Russia, Japan, Mexico, Romania, Israel, and Canada), who were hand-picked to meet on our stage in Powell Hall. This group of one hundred or more men and women are nurturing and then passing on to audiences in St. Louis, and in many of the important cities of Europe and Asia, a legacy that hundreds before them have contributed. To me, their music is like an eloquent sermon.

While standing up for our orchestra's bow after a concert during our 1997 winter subscription series, I looked around at my smiling colleagues and was very touched by what I saw. There were many old friends who had given so much to our joint musical effort over the years, but more than seventy percent of the musicians I was looking at had joined us since I had arrived. Many of these young players were already in leadership roles. There were many more young-uns among us. As usually happens in organizations like the Saint Louis Symphony, the turnovers seem to occur in waves. The Symphony was in the middle of one of those waves.

These waves of young people were continually and enthusiastically searching for the truth, often diplomatically. Alison Harney, who is the Symphony's principal second violinist, once asked me, "John, what do you think of doing it all in one bow at four after letter C?" She didn't fool me for a second. I knew what she was really thinking: "Why is John taking two bows there; it sounds so stupid breaking up the phrase like that." But I let her diplomacy win me over and never let on that I was on to her strategy.

These young people seem to have brought with them such an atmosphere of great enthusiasm and the ability to be team players that I felt that they were transforming the Symphony right in front of my eyes and ears. It seems to me that the Symphony was soaring higher with every week that went by and that it was performing at the highest level I had heard since joining the Symphony over forty years ago. If I had not been a little uneasy with all these young whippersnappers breathing down my neck, I could have just relaxed and let them do my job, which they thought they were so good at. Sometimes they were positively annoying.

Alvin McCall, one of the cellists in my section and someone who was obviously carrying on the tradition of Marilyn Beabout, found everything that could possibly be questionable about the printed music we were playing. He bugged the heck out of me until a satisfactory explanation was forthcoming from either me or the conductor. If Alvin were not such a great cellist, I would have suggested that he become a conductor himself and stop bothering me.

Often the rest of the section would roll their eyes as Alvin started on one of his search-and-destroy missions, looking for a possible misprint in the score. Usually he was on to something, and it was worth the effort to listen to him. He was so effective at finding errors in the printed pages that, on occasion, certain people in the orchestra, with questionable motives, had used his skills to their advantage. These people, knowing full well what was going to happen, encouraged Alvin to ask a guest conductor one of his complicated questions. There was only five minutes left in the rehearsal. Everyone was dead tired from a very hard session and not anxious to press another finger down or blow another breath into his mouthpiece. Alvin obliged these people by asking one of his typically convoluted questions. The orchestra members settled back in their chairs for a nice rest. Not only did we not play again that day, but also we almost went into overtime as the guest conductor tried to answer Alvin's inquiry.

Sometimes I jokingly protested, "Alvin, you are going to make me lose my job, showing me up like this. You are always finding mistakes before me." Sometimes he stretched this whole thing a little far, and we all enjoyed it when he was kidded about it.

Once, during a rehearsal, he was pestering me about the fact that there was no *piano* written in a certain part of the music. We were, in fact, already playing softly at this spot in question. It seemed obvious to most of us, in spite of the missing directions, that this was the thing to do. Alvin knew that too, and I was sure that he was doing the same as the rest of us. He felt that he had a musicological point in his mind that needed to be resolved. He was looking at the big picture, so he kept up the nagging. I pleaded, "Oh Alvin, don't make me bother Vonk about this one!" The maestro noticed the discussion going on beneath him and decided, probably against his better judgment, to consider the question.

As I relayed the situation to our director, I began to see some merit in Alvin's question. Vonk, after straightening things out and answering Alvin's question, looked down at his score and spoke quietly and so slowly that there may have been a full second between some of the words: "Yes, but (pause) it's (pause) a (pause) bit (pause) far (pause) fetched."

How sweet that was. See, those newcomers weren't that smart.

CHAPTER

56

YO YO MAHVELOUS

If you know anything about the music business, I'm sure that you know who Yo Yo Ma is. He is one of the best cellists in the world. It might be interesting to note here that we studied with the same teacher, Leonard Rose. I guess that Yo Yo was a better listener. In fact, Yo Yo is a good listener. For someone so famous, who has done so much for music and musicians, and who is an artist to whom the world listens, he actually listens to everybody else. He even listens to me.

Whenever Yo Yo came to be a soloist with the Saint Louis Symphony, the first thing he did at the initial rehearsal, when he came onstage with his cello in one hand, was to walk past his special soloist chair over to me. He would then shake my hand with his other hand and ask me how my daughter Sara was. Then he would listen to me brag about her. He even looked as though he was interested in what I was saying.

I'm sure that there are a thousand stories out there about Yo Yo's humility and his kindness to fellow musicians and to young cello students. After concerts, I've seen him take the time to chat with every aspiring young musician who crowded around him in the Green Room. That's the special room where visiting artists warm up and, after their performances, greet their many fans. He even let some kids play a few notes on his magnificent Stradivarius. Watching that scene made me jealous, but I thought that it might be gauche for me to butt in.

Yo Yo can play good-natured jokes on you. He teased me during one of his solo appearances with us. I didn't even realize what he was doing until my assistant principal cellist, Cathy Lehr, tapped me on the shoulder and asked, "John, do you know what Yo Yo is doing?"

Well, I knew Yo Yo had been looking around and smiling at me while he was playing a cadenza in his solo concerto, but I couldn't for the life of me figure out why. Then Cathy whispered to me, "He's improvising and putting that piece you played yesterday in your recital into his cadenza."

First of all, how the heck did he just stick that music into his cadenza at the last minute and still play it better than I did? Darn!

Okay, Yo Yo Ma is great—rah, rah, rah—but in one way I am better than he is. I'll explain.

One day I came early to a rehearsal, as I usually did, to warm up. I often went out to the lobby, where it was less noisy than on the stage, to practice. When I opened the door, however, I saw that there were four hundred people sitting there listening to some sounds coming from a platform at the other end of the lobby. "Darn, I'll have to warm up on the stage after all," I thought.

No, I couldn't do that because the piano tuner was on the stage, and I knew that he didn't want to hear a cellist playing scales. "All right, I'll go into the Green Room and practice my Bach *Cello Suite No. 5* there, before the rest of the orchestra arrives."

Even better, there was a special cello chair in the room and a stand for my music. So I sat down and started sawing away. It wasn't until I was half way through the suite, which I was trying to memorize, that I realized that I was actually in Yo Yo's warm-up room. I had forgotten that Yo Yo was our soloist that week. I froze. I didn't want the great Yo Yo to come in and hear me scrubbing away on my cello. But then I said to myself, "Don't be a coward. Finish what you are playing."

Well, just as I finished, in he walks, and being the caring person he is, he asked what music I was playing. See, he cared. When I told him and mentioned how it was challenging for me to memorize those thousands of notes, he said, "Hey, come up to my room after the concert tonight, and I'll show you how I try to approach it."

Just then the personnel manager came up to us and asked if I would go on the radio for Yo Yo, as he had to warm up for the rehearsal. Then I figured out what the crowd in the lobby was doing. They were listening to Yo Yo doing a radio interview.

"Sure! I'll step in for him." I knew I would do a great job.

The first question the interviewer asked me was what did I, as the first cellist of SLSO, think of Yo Yo. I quickly responded, "Yo Yo is great, but I am better."

I'm sure that the jaws of the four hundred people in the audience dropped, just as the interviewer's did, until I added, "I've lost my cello three times, and Yo Yo has lost his only once."

CHAPTER

57

WHO'S THE BEST?

For thirty-five years I had the honor, or
pressure—you decide, of being a member of the
Symphony's audition committee. Usually ten of us
orchestra members would sit on the stage of
Powell Hall and try to determine which of the sixty
to one hundred candidates performing for us
behind a giant screen should be invited to join our
orchestra. Sixty hopeful musicians would often be
trying out for just one vacancy. If you want to talk
about pressure, that was it. Yes, the candidates
must have felt pretty pressured as well: Each was
allowed only five minutes in the preliminaries to
impress us as he or she played part of a solo
concerto and a few excerpts from difficult
orchestral music. As a judge, however, I may have
felt more pressure than all the candidates put
together. "Oh, Lord, help me make the right
decision" was the prayer that I think a lot of us
were reciting silently.

Frankly, I think that it wasn't as hard fifty years ago as it is today for an audition committee to decide who is the best candidate. Why? There simply were not as many whiz kids out there then. Why more now? Partly because music schools all over the country are graduating larger classes, and partly because a new method of teaching has evolved since the "good old days." Simply put, more teachers are using the empowerment approach, as opposed to the harsh, critical technique that Beethoven's father employed.

With all those talented kids out there now, what are audition committees looking for? Well, it goes without saying that a "wannabe" symphonic musician had better have great rhythm and be able to play in tune; read Italian well enough to follow the directions of the composer; and get his fingers to move fast enough to chop out most of the notes on the page put in front of him. Most important of all, I think that he must be able to produce a beautiful sound, or I should say, a gorgeous sound—a sound that touches your soul.

What's amazing is that there is not one particular sound that we can label number one. Each sound produced by a fine musician is totally different from that of any other musician. This is true even if two musicians take turns playing on the same instrument, as my daughter Sara and I will often do on the same cello. Each musician's sound is as different as each human voice is different. Can you recognize a friend's voice from behind a screen? I'm sure you can.

I have recognized the violin sound of a friend when he or she was playing behind a screen. No, I did not tell anyone on the audition committee until after the player was chosen for the finals, which were held after the screen came down. So, there.

What makes a tone beautiful? Purity and volume have got to be there. There is also vibrato. Vibrato is the gentle vibrating of the pitch from a note to a slightly lower pitch and back, sometimes fast, sometimes slow, sometimes wide, sometimes narrow. Vibrato affects the ear of the listener in such a magical way that it behooves any aspiring string musician to pick up a box of vibrato powder at their nearest Wal-Mart.

Seriously, if a musician is using the right vibrato combined with the right intensity and volume of sound appropriate for the music being played at that particular moment, then he or she can win the prize anytime—unless there is more than one applicant who touches your soul with his or her beautiful sound. If so, start praying, "Oh, Lord, help me make the right decision."

CHAPTER

58

ANOTHER NEWCOMER

As much as every orchestra member, past and present, has contributed to the Saint Louis Symphony's legacy, we should also acknowledge the importance of many non-musicians. Without their love, devotion, and financial support, the SLSO wouldn't be able to turn on the lights in Powell Hall. Even though the SLSO is not a financially profitable business, it is a noble one.

During my tenure with the Symphony, we had some great symphony boards and wonderful board presidents. They, along with the executive director of the orchestra, received a lot of stress and not much glory. They kept us alive and fed. In 1997 we were blessed to have, at an incredibly challenging time for classical music in general, and more specifically, for symphony orchestras, two brilliant and imaginative leaders who ran the show upstairs: Bruce Coppock, Executive Director, and John W. Bachman, Chairman of the Symphony Board. They have left their legacies to us just as many other illustrious St. Louis citizens had over the past one hundred thirty years.

The argument could be made that those who have left the greatest part of themselves with the Symphony, or molded its persona the most, were its conductors, past and present. It's easy for me to see how those former music directors under whom I served, Charles Münch and Erich Leinsdorf in Boston, and Walter Susskind, Jerzy Semkow, Leonard Slatkin, Hans Vonk, Itzhak Perlman, and David Robertson in St. Louis, brought something special to each orchestra. Each conductor was unique. Each conductor's gift to his institution was different, but invaluable. It's tempting to compare them, but I won't. Judging musicians of the rank of symphonic music directors is extremely subjective. Anyway, comparisons in this case are not only odious, but also unreliable.

Orchestra members may dislike a conductor whom the audience adores and the critics are so neutral about that they forget to talk about him; they talk instead about the composers or the weather in their reviews.

One of the Saint Louis Symphony's maestros, Hans Vonk, had been with the orchestra for only a short time, but his impact on it had been awesome. An orchestra is a little like Henry VIII and his wives: We move quickly from the recently departed to the next one and enjoy the new collaboration to the fullest. He was loved and respected by the orchestra members. I think that his being Dutch is one reason we had bonded so quickly. His humor was quite similar to ours, if perhaps a little drier. At rehearsals he used it very effectively to relieve tension, which he created in his quest for perfection. The following illustrates this point.

At the end of one of our rehearsals, David Halen, our concertmaster, came up to me as I was talking to Vonk and said, "I still like the sixteenth note better in that spot." I quickly agreed with him, and then we chattered enthusiastically for a minute or so about how we were of the same mind on this very important issue, while the maestro quietly listened to our conversation. All of a sudden, it became apparent that we were talking about two different pieces. We paused, embarrassed, not sure where we should go with this discussion.

The maestro quickly filled the silence by remarking, "This is wonderful; you two gentlemen can agree on completely different things."

Hans Vonk was as much into "control-magic" as Ormandy and the rest of them, but he applied it so gradually that you didn't see it coming. As the weeks went by, I saw that he was pulling us into his web and that it was futile to resist. He had been sneaking up on us and zapping us with such small doses that we didn't feel it at first, but he wasn't fooling me. I had been around too long not to see what he was doing. I was only too happy to fill everyone in.

Vonk was both a perfectionist and a pragmatist. He was an idealist, he was also human. During a rehearsal, the maestro would seem deeply concerned and very intense as he reached for a particular goal in the music that some would say was unobtainable. When he didn't reach it, his shoulders might droop, and yes, you might even see the disappointment in his face. This in itself would spell disaster for all involved if he didn't apply a little magic. Many a conductor doing the same thing has lost an orchestra because the musicians will soon become very cautious. Fearing the director's displeasure, they avoid the risk of exposing themselves and going for the brass ring.

Vonk would relax for an instant and give the impression that he understood how hard it was and that he appreciated our effort. His demands, accompanied by his understanding, did the trick. This would happen over and over again, and each time the musicians invested more. We saw what he wanted and were not afraid to risk everything. He got what he wanted little by little, day by day, and so on. Vonk's conception was always growing.

Vonk left nothing to chance. Everything had to be in its right place: "The cellos must be soft so the flutes can come out; the bassoon must end the phrase here, so strings beware." His conception grew daily. You were surprised at the heights that could be attained. His communication skills would be the envy of the best marriage counselor. He needed them because he was constantly imparting information to us, saving his wonderful baton technique for the concerts.

Listening to someone impart information can be extremely boring. It is the first dangerous moment in the rehearsal. Here he was so clever. When he wanted to fix something, he stopped us with his time-out hand signal, hesitating a moment, as if he were searching for the right words to express an important point. This made us anxious to hear what he was going to say. We became children waiting for their father to get on with a bedtime story. He may have been actually searching for words in English, since he was Dutch, but who cared. It was that magic again, and you were being caught in his web.

By the time we arrived at the concert, he had things pretty much under control. You would think he could have started to relax then, but he didn't. He took his baton out of its scabbard and went to work. Now the tension really started to build. Constantly pivoting on the podium, he seemed to be facing every member of the orchestra at once as he reached for the brass ring. Those of us who were close to him could hear his constant groaning, which indicated that he was definitely involved. The maestro built tension in a hundred different ways, but his effective use of tempo relationships was probably one of his most impressive skills. The music always seemed to be moving forward or easing off. Nothing was static.

To do this, of course, he had to have everyone's complete cooperation. If you veered from the course that he was setting, the mood was ruined. His excellent baton technique usually kept us in line, but sometimes we drifted a little. Not for long, though, because his face, which went into an alarm mode, and his eyes, which became quite large as he focused them on the culprits, hurried the wayward ones back into the fold immediately. Because he had showed his humanity during rehearsals, most took no offense at these faces. We understood that it was an emergency. We moved on as Vonk focused all his attention on us and the music until the final cadence.

Though the maestro never seemed to be aware of the audience members, they got their money's worth. His humility showed as he acknowledged their appreciation. When he turned to us to show his gratitude for our efforts, I'm sure that I have seen him slip some of that leftover magic into his pocket for the next rehearsal. How else could he have done it?

CHAPTER

59

A MAN CALLED HENRY

There is so much to see when you look at an orchestra with its one hundred members. Most important, you are seeing a living, growing organism that is constantly striving to express "truth." What is this truth? I think that Mozart's *Symphony No. 29* is one truth. The extraordinary group of men and women in a symphony orchestra will express it for you. They are able to do this at any given moment, even without rehearsal, because of all that has come before. Each individual performance is built not only on the latest conductor's input, but also on other maestros' contributions, which remain with these wonderful musicians for the rest of their lives.

It is probable that many conductors have left their marks on the Saint Louis Symphony as we grew as an orchestra. This impetus for growth came from the Symphony's musicians, and the daily experience of hearing magnificent solos by our principal players was inspiring to us all. As individuals, they set standards for us as a group. In fact, every Symphony musician, past and present, has had the opportunity to affect the whole and has made the Symphony a better expression of the truth.

Something I find so interesting is how much symphony orchestras have changed over the years and how differently rehearsals are run today. Fifty years ago, I played a rehearsal with the BSO that Leopold Stokowski conducted. He was famous for never allowing time for his musicians to find their places in the music after he had stopped and corrected them. He would begin beating again at exactly the same time as he told them where to start. "Five after B," he'd say, and he was already on the sixth bar. Of course, only a few ever started there, and the rest of the orchestra members, many of whom were still writing his instructions into their music, would have to scramble aboard as best they could. I thought it was the funniest thing I'd ever seen, and I said that to my stand-partner. The next thing I knew, I was called into the personnel manager's office and told that the maestro, who I didn't think even knew I was in his orchestra, way back on the last stand, had seen me talking, and he wanted it to stop. Stokowski had the best "control-magic" I'd ever seen. He was also an example of the kind of autocracy that, thank goodness, is fading away today.

Orchestras are not, at least during concerts and rehearsals, democracies. Yet there is a spirit in the air that makes the musicians' lives a lot more pleasant. It was unheard of back then that a player on the last stand would pop up in rehearsal and ask a question of the conductor. In the Saint Louis Symphony, however, Tom LeVeck changed all that. Being naturally curious, and tired of passing his questions up through the second violin section and waiting five minutes for an answer, he tried the direct approach. One day Tom blurted out in a loud voice from the back of the orchestra, "Maestro, are we supposed to play forte at letter R?"

The first time he asked a question this way, the guest conductor looked at me in surprise. I quickly said, "He's independently wealthy," to explain his precedent-setting brashness. Nowadays, many players from all over the orchestra ask questions. I think it usually saves time, though not everyone is convinced yet. Sometimes Vonk would call time-out with that famous referee's hand signal and say, "No more questions; we've got to get through." The musicians generally use this new freedom discreetly. It reflects another important change occurring among the section players in orchestras today. They don't look at themselves as being simply cogs in a wheel; they see themselves as caring team players who have more to contribute in expressing the truth than just their gift for synchronized playing.

There is definitely a shift in attitude occurring. Where did it all start? I don't know about other orchestras, but I do know where most of it started in the Saint Louis Symphony. It was in the heart and mind of one of the grandest gentlemen who ever put on the uniform of black tails and patent leather shoes. His name was Henry.

Henry Loew was principal bass of the Saint Louis Symphony for close to fifty years, and his legacy will always be remembered. He single-handedly changed the way the musicians in the Symphony, and many others in other orchestras around the country, looked at themselves. Just as important, he changed how management, boards, and conductors looked at the musicians.

In the early 1950s, Henry, along with some other brave orchestra members, started the Saint Louis Symphony Orchestra committee, which was the first of its kind in the country and a model for the rest of the nation. By the mid-1950s, several other symphonies had established orchestra committees modeled after the Saint Louis Symphony Orchestra committee. When Henry arrived in Cleveland for a general meeting of the committees, he walked into a standing ovation.

Until Henry, along with his brave friends, Russell Brodine and Richard O'Donnell, started the unheard of concept of orchestra members being able to speak with their maestros, the musicians were working mostly at the pleasure of their conductors, managers, and symphony boards. They had little protection against being fired and were not in a position to ask for better working conditions. Henry had to endure the scorn of many—even the scorn of some of the other orchestra members—who could not understand his noble motives. He was labeled a pinko and a troublemaker.

In spite of all this, Henry continued to be long-suffering and patient. He lovingly held to his convictions by patiently turning the other cheek. He never let go of his dream of an orchestra in which each musician would have pride in himself.

Henry worked to draw out information vital to the progress of all the Symphony musicians from sources that tried to withhold it for their own interests. I was told that he was instrumental in the founding of ICSOM, The International Conference of Symphony and Opera Musicians, which had its first meeting in St. Louis. It was to revolutionize the orchestra world in the United States. I believe that he also started, with Russell Brodine, the Association of Personnel Managers.

Henry became the single most beloved man in the Saint Louis Symphony. Even all his past sins against the powers that be were eventually forgiven. His compassion for his colleagues and his students was legendary.

In 1965 he was recognized by the tough but astute Executive Director Peter Pastreich as the perfect choice to be the personnel manager of the Symphony. Henry, at first, refused the offer, but Peter, who was later to become the Executive Director of the San Francisco Symphony, knew that only Henry had the grace and understanding to work with all sides. Although it took six months to get Henry to agree, Peter wouldn't take no for an answer. Henry didn't let Peter or the musicians down. He healed hurts and brought everyone together.

Henry never stopped healing people or problems until the day he died in 1996, three years after he retired. He always had time for everyone and healed so many of us with his love. Beginning in 1958 Henry taught the attitude that is now prevalent at and integral to the Saint Louis Symphony: It's a joy to come to work.

Henry Loew was a great father to his children and a great husband to his wonderful wife, Mildred. He was an accordionist, a therapist, a mediator, and a comedian (with his daily joke). He was a great teacher, a great friend, a great personnel manager of the Symphony, and finally, a great principal bassist. This was a lot for one man to be, but there was one thing that Henry wasn't.

Joe Kleeman, the Symphony's then associate personnel manager and Henry's friend for more than forty years, told me this story, which occurred many years ago. Henry had just finished playing a bass recital in which he had programmed the Koussevitzky, Hindemith, and Dragonetti bass concertos along with some movements of the Bach cello suites.

The next evening, Henry asked Joe if he would come with him to his synagogue. Joe was happy to go along with his friend, but was surprised when, during their singing of the hymns, he heard Henry's voice wandering all over the place. Joe said, "Henry, last night you just finished playing one of the hardest programs of music a bassist can put together, and you played it brilliantly. What's happening to you? How can you get lost in these simple hymns, singing half notes and whole notes?"

Easy. Henry couldn't sing.

CHAPTER

60

ALL IN THE FAMILY

In the early part of April 1997, a great deal of pressure was building up in Powell Hall as the Symphony prepared for a very important performance, which it was to give in New York City in three weeks. This Carnegie Hall performance was to be the first opportunity for the New York critics to judge the quality of the collaboration between the new maestro, Hans Vonk, and the Saint Louis Symphony. Everyone was hoping for perfection. That can make people a little jumpy. What happened during those few weeks should be viewed with compassion and understanding for all involved.

It is hard to know exactly how all the commotion started. Perhaps our maestro expressed some momentary frustration, common to all perfectionists, with a particular player's performance of a particular passage in a particular piece of music, which we were soon to perform in New York.

When a symphony management is working with a new music director, it is not uncommon for individuals within the management staff to be a little overanxious to please. (The same situation could occur within a large business corporation.) When a musically-based decision affecting a musician is made, the results can sometimes be explosive. Such a decision can be damaging; the timing can be even more damaging, especially when it appears to skirt union and traditional rules. The morale of a whole orchestra can be adversely affected and then be reflected in the symphonic output. The timing, in this case, was the worst possible—just before the all-important New York concert. Since the union contract would not have allowed the sudden removal of a player in the middle of the season, there was a great deal of effort needed by the management to persuade the musician in question to take a leave of absence to allow the Symphony to bring in someone else as a replacement. One can only assume that it went something like this: "It would be in the best interest of the orchestra if you would step down for a few weeks until after the Carnegie Hall concert is over."

Guilt is a very powerful weapon when used on a conscientious person. Our esteemed colleague reluctantly agreed to management's request, and the news of the proposed personnel change began spreading through the orchestra while it was on a

Missouri tour. An orchestra can feel disjointed when away from its home base. At first we musicians were confused as to what we should collectively do at a time like this.

Communicating was difficult. We were not even sure that our colleague wanted to return after what seemed like unbearable pressure was used to bring about his temporary removal. Soon it became clear to all of us that we would not be the Saint Louis Symphony without our colleague. We didn't want to appear in Carnegie Hall minus that player. We were unanimous in thinking that there needed to be a full orchestra meeting, once we returned to St. Louis, to address the problem.

That Monday morning meeting in the spring of 1997 turned out to be five hours long. It was extraordinary in many ways. We didn't know it then, but the events that ensued reinforced my notion that a key factor in the strength and health of a symphony orchestra is that all major decisions must be ethical and moral. This situation, just before the New York concert and in the face of the Symphony's steep financial challenges, may very well have shaped the course of the orchestra's future. The subject of this fateful meeting was originally never to be made public because it was an internal matter. All concerned, musicians, management, and conductor alike, felt that no one outside the Symphony family needed to know what was going on. Unfortunately the local papers caught wind of the unpopular musical decision and how it was being handled. It was a shame that journalists were able to report only the hurt, but not how the hurt was healed so beautifully by the whole family.

I'll try to do that here, to explain how the healing strengthened the success of the orchestra. The Symphony did not believe that disclosing the nature of the challenge was important. Everyone believed that what had happened was simply a mistake, though a serious one. What was important was the chance for all of us to witness a group of men and women pulling together to resolve an issue in a manner that would have made Henry proud and would perhaps set a precedent for other orchestras around the country.

Everyone who attended that meeting came away emotionally drained, in awe of the solidarity and the desire for honest reconciliation demonstrated by our unique symphony orchestra. Many of us shed tears of gratitude on seeing the love and concern expressed by everyone for our colleague, who was in a tough situation. Our younger members, who had never seen their orchestra spring into action like this, were duly impressed and quickly added their important support.

It was definitely a time of bonding. Even our maestro, the day after the meeting, was invited to join our orchestra family discussion. His acceptance of our offer was, I am sure, a first for any conductor. It was, I am also sure, a first for a music director to cancel part of his important rehearsal so that he could address his orchestra, take any blame for all misunderstandings, and then work to find a solution to the family's dilemma.

The Saint Louis Symphony had been my second family for almost thirty years, and I loved it. My real family and my orchestra family have been enmeshed with each other over a period of eighty-two years. My father played the violin in the Symphony in 1928. I joined the Symphony in 1968, and both my daughters started playing with the Symphony as extras in the early 1980s, while they were still in high school. When I injured my arm, my daughter Sara replaced me in a solo performance of the Schumann *Cello Concerto.*

I think that this warm feeling that I have for our Symphony is shared by most of my colleagues, and perhaps more than anything else, it is the reason we sounded so good, if I may be so bold. A loving, healthy family has a wonderful aura about it; this blesses all who come near it. It's the same with an orchestra. An orchestra that is happy plays with its whole heart and soul, and this can create only great music.

If ever that fantasy of mine, in which we bring the world's great orchestras together for a symphonic Super Bowl, becomes a reality, we will have to create an all-star team as well. I'm positive that the SLSO would be well represented. We would certainly have players who would be equal to players from Boston, Philadelphia, and Berlin.

But no orchestra has them all. If an orchestra did have them all, it would not necessarily make it a great orchestra. Remember our cello section in the BSO, which had all the stars for a short time, but that, in my opinion, didn't sound as good as the old-timers?

Though every member of a great orchestra has to be pretty darn good to win and pass the many necessary auditions before being invited aboard, every orchestra is made up of musicians of diverse talents and skills. I see this diversity not as a defect, but as an asset. I had been the first cellist in the Saint Louis Symphony, but I had to recognize that there had been cellists in my section who could have, at times, played more brilliantly than I could, or at least were superior at counting rests. This does not demean me or make me less of a musician. In fact, by recognizing this, I improved as I worked in this area. Others may have learned from me in an area in which I was stronger. This process happens throughout any orchestra, as the musicians pull together to produce their beautiful music.

I'm convinced that diversity in age is an asset in an organization like the Saint Louis Symphony. Older musicians can be good role models; more than half of the SLSO principal players could have been classified as mature. I've also seen older colleagues grow and improve as the younger players surrounded them with their enthusiasm. I wanted to be such an older player. The ability of a mature person to outdo himself and break the limitations that society would impose on him is probably best seen in the musician's world. Though being seventy years old might keep you off a professional football league's all-star team, it definitely would not hurt your chances at making the symphony all-stars. Seventy-year-old all-stars can light the path for the younger generation. In 2009 Roger Kaza, my old sailing buddy, won the principal horn position in the Symphony, competing against many much younger musicians.

At some time we all get tricked into becoming perfectionists in our approach to music making, and then the essence of what we do begins to suffer. Conductors and orchestra members alike never stop striving to reach the goal of musical perfection. We continually hope that perhaps "today is the day," but more important, we try never to lose sight of the fact that our hearts and souls are what make it all possible.

All these and many other insights that occurred during our five-hour orchestra meeting helped the musicians, the conductor, and management to conclude that our threatened colleague should not be allowed to leave us. We needed him too badly.

This, however, did not take off the pressure that was building on all of us. We wanted to do well for the upcoming Carnegie concert. We wondered what effect the temporary squabble was going to have on our music making. Was our maestro going to lose control of his musicians? Was our returning principal player going to be troubled by the whole world watching? Were players going to stay angry or, even worse, become cautious, which would destroy all that we had built so far? We had no way of knowing, but I could see that we had some heroes among us.

The orchestra had acted heroically because it refused to take a confrontational stance to solve the problem. It was a healing approach. Henry Loew and all his brave friends, who paved the way for us fifty years ago, would have been proud of their colleagues that Monday morning. Hans Vonk was a hero because he refused to allow anyone else to take responsibility for the mistake and reversed the decision, for the greater good. That would not have been easy for any conductor. I never thought that I would see it in my day. Vonk also never stopped trying to bring the best out in us for those next two weeks before the New York concert. He didn't become cautious. He didn't change. He seemed totally unaffected by the whole chaotic situation—as did the individual musician.

Nevertheless, the question was still there. How was all this going to play out at Carnegie Hall?

Stay tuned.

CHAPTER

61

THE REHEARSAL

Most musicians in the Saint Louis Symphony were not born yesterday. We knew, as well as everyone else, that a great part of an orchestra's national and international reputation is built on the stage of that magnificent Carnegie Hall, in front of the discriminating New York audiences and the even more discriminating New York critics.

After seventeen years of successful Carnegie concerts with Leonard Slatkin, that concert on Wednesday evening, April 24, 1997, was to be our first appearance with our new music director, Hans Vonk. The whole music world would be watching. I'm not privy to all the machinations that go on behind the scenes in the orchestra management business, but I would bet my cello that recording contracts, prospects for national and international tours, state and government grants, and general financial support from whomever, were going to be affected by the impression that we would made at our New York debut. Is this a gigantic amount of pressure for an orchestra and a conductor? I think so.

There was a lot at stake. To add to the equation, we had all been through some traumatic moments in meeting the challenge with our respected colleague. Had we all forgiven and forgotten? Or did we still, as the therapists say, have a lot of anger. Or maybe worse, were we now overly cautious or downright scared to play with the abandon necessary to pull off the big one? An orchestra doesn't hit the jackpot without having some freedom in its playing. We all knew what we were aiming for; we just didn't know what kind of ammunition we still had left.

During those tense two weeks before the concert, I was reminded of a similar situation that occurred when I was still in Boston. The BSO's conductor, Erich Leinsdorf, tried to demote the orchestra's principal brass player to second chair and replace him with another musician from New York, just before one of the BSO's Carnegie Hall concerts. The best that I can remember is that members of the BSO had been upset by this inappropriate mid-season personnel change and threatened a strike, forcing Leinsdorf to reverse his edict. It seemed to many of us in the orchestra that Leinsdorf never recovered from his loss of face over the incident. His effectiveness as the BSO's music director suffered from that time forward. The SLSO certainly did not want to repeat that scenario. I always felt that Erich Leinsdorf was far more effective as a guest conductor with the Saint Louis Symphony than he was as music director in Boston. With the SLSO, there was no past.

That afternoon nerves were on edge as we began to rehearse Bruckner's monumental *Symphony No. 7* for that evening's Carnegie Hall performance. Vonk, who in a sense was one of us now and seemingly unaffected by the drama of the past two weeks, rolled up his sleeves and asked us for more than he had previously. Most conductors at a dress rehearsal like this would have left well enough alone, touched on a few tricky spots, and then dismissed us with a few words of encouragement, such as, "See you all tonight. It will be great, and have a good supper." Not Hans.

"Winds, you are never with us on that rallentando. Violins, that's too aggressive at letter L. That's not what the composer intended." He wouldn't stop striving for perfection. Tension was mounting. All this was happening in front of an audience of Saint Louis Symphony donors, who had been invited to see and hear a live rehearsal in Carnegie Hall. This probably didn't make our maestro too comfortable, because his extremely demanding rehearsal technique was not something he wanted non-musicians to see. Gradually, certain principal players were becoming agitated as they, too, demanded more from themselves and, occasionally, from each other. Tempers began to flare, and some of us thought for a moment that our orchestral family was going to explode right there on the stage. Several days later one of our colleagues quipped, "Did you read the review of our Wednesday rehearsal in the sports page?"

Vonk grew silent. For the first time that I could remember, he actually looked angry. For a brief moment he was not in his usual good-natured mood. Nobody moved or said a word. The concertmaster, David Halen, and I exchanged glances that seemed to say, "Let's hope we all get out of this alive." There was more silence. I know I shouldn't have tried to read Vonk's mind, but it looked as if he was thinking to himself, "How did we get into this mess?"

He paused, looked around at the audience that he probably wished wasn't witnessing this, and then turned back to us. For a moment he said nothing. We all sat holding onto our seats, waiting for his next move. His look of anger gave way to one of frustration. He glanced at the score, again at the audience, and finally back at us. Then he said that word. It was the only word that was fitting for the moment, the one that could truly express our feelings as we tried, with all our hearts, to do justice to Bruckner's masterpiece, but found ourselves temporarily off track. You know the word. It rhymes with "fit," has four letters, and your mother washed your mouth out with soap if you ever used it. The maestro was spared the soap, but he got one hundred men and women on the stage to laugh and, finally, to relax. He said this word so quietly that the audience never heard it, and we didn't tell.

With that one word Vonk broke the tension. He also broke through a wall that seemed to be preventing us from accomplishing what we knew we could do. Vonk smiled, but didn't let up. He renewed his efforts to get as much out of us as he could, and he kept demanding until the last second of the rehearsal. We gave him what he asked for. That night we all went on the stage with a love for Bruckner that helped us carry the evening. It felt as though we had won that famous brass ring. All the energy that had been building up for the last three weeks poured out into a performance that was truly memorable. At least that's what the discriminating New York audiences and the even more discriminating New York critics seemed to be telling us with their standing ovations and glowing reviews. As we musicians walked back to our hotel rooms after the concert, we felt very proud to be members of the SLSO family.

Reviewer Bernard Holland wrote in *The New York Times* on Friday, April 25, 1997: "If Hans Vonk and the members of the St. Louis Symphony are not yet celebrating their mutual good fortune, they should start. The Dutch conductor and new music director in St. Louis has long been busy with Europe's orchestras, but one doubts he has ever had firmly in his hands a group of this accomplishment."

CHAPTER

62

OUR FIRST CHALLENGE

In 2002 the orchestra members of the Saint Louis Symphony were notified that there was to be an important meeting regarding their future. For months we had been hearing rumors of the impending doom. We were reading numerous articles in the *St. Louis Post-Dispatch* as well as in the national press about the hopelessness of our Symphony's situation.

For a number of years the Symphony had been running huge deficits, draining funds from its small endowments and going deeper and deeper into debt. The Symphony was facing bankruptcy. The day of the famous meeting finally arrived, and our greatest fears were realized. This was perhaps the lowest point in the history of the second oldest orchestra in the United States.

Most of us were in despair as we headed home that evening after the meeting. We all faced the prospect of reduced salaries, lost pensions, shortened seasons, and reduced orchestra size—

all of which would have an impact on our lives as well as on all of St. Louis's other music lovers. But that day was probably the starting point for an inspiring rescue operation to save what I considered to be the most important institution that our great city would ever possess.

I believe that a symphony orchestra is a metaphor for life. It's made up of one hundred people who are as diverse as you can get. It has men and women of different ages and of different cultural, religious, and political backgrounds, and it encompasses every imaginable temperament. All of these people must work together and bring the fruit of their labors to an eager public, and they do it all under one god (well, sometimes it seems as if a conductor thinks that he is a god). An orchestra is the most telling example of what can happen when people work together in harmony to reach an objective that touches all those around them.

The symbolism is striking. If humanity could put aside, even momentarily, all self interest to work together for a common goal, as every member of a symphony orchestra does, peace and harmony would reign in our world.

But would our precious Saint Louis Symphony survive?

After that frightening meeting, things began to happen. The team began to work together like it never did before. The team consisted of the orchestra members, the symphony administration and staff, the board, local journalists, the music counsel, St. Louis's corporate heads, the union, the special orchestra negotiating committee, and the citizens of St. Louis. They all began to focus on one thing—saving our jewel. Their efforts brought praise from the press all around the country. Soon it appeared that the Saint Louis Symphony would survive for another one hundred fifty years and at the same artistic levels it had always enjoyed.

How they got it done is material for another book. It is important, however, to note several factors that contributed to the results, which many other orchestras in similar situations long to duplicate.

One highly respected community leader, Jack Taylor, founder of Enterprise Auto Leasing (now Enterprise Rent-A-Car), stepped forward with a huge matching grant of forty million dollars, which started the ball rolling. (By the way, please rent their cars.)

Our dedicated chairman of the Symphony board, Virginia Weldon, daringly appointed a new executive director, Randy Adams, who knew little about music. His contacts in the corporate world, however, would eventually enable the Symphony to raise more money, in a short time, than it ever had before in its history.

Even before that fateful meeting occurred, our negotiating committee, which comprised five brilliant Saint Louis Symphony musicians, each in possession of an incredibly imaginative mind, began working around the clock to come up with different possibilities for everyone to consider. The negotiating committee was guiding the orchestra members and the administration along the path to solutions rather than to doom and gloom. The committee was getting us to concentrate on working together to solve our challenges rather than retreating to our own castles. Maybe we each had to give a little here and there.

A very important ingredient in the formula for a solution was a journalist, Sara Bryan Miller, of the *St. Louis Post Dispatch*, who never stopped writing articles about the situation and kept the Symphony constantly in the news, often on the front page.

Another important ingredient was that several of the board members began to come forward with very large gifts specifically targeted to prevent the musicians' salaries from being lowered more than a moderate amount. Of course, there were my talented colleagues, who agreed to allow the board to breach the union contract and renegotiate new terms. There was also generous help from the audiences, the general public, and even from people who had never attended a concert.

It was truly everyone working together that saved us. This team saved an institution that brought true beauty to the world. No one gave up. No one became immobilized. No one stopped talking to those around town or across the table from them. In the wake of the threat we all faced, very few musicians left for other positions. Most stayed and worked to prevail. For years I had seen many of our young musicians leave us to go to higher positions in other orchestras, often returning to even higher positions with us. That was normal for any orchestra. But during our most challenging time, when you would have thought that all of the musicians would have been tempted to exit, only two players left. This kept the Saint Louis Symphony basically intact and ready to provide the same beautiful product that its audiences had grown accustomed to for more than one hundred years. It had been a time when no one wanted to leave the team.

CHAPTER

63

OUR SECORD CHALLENGE

At the same time, in the midst of all the stress and turmoil that the Saint Louis Symphony was experiencing because of the looming financial crisis, another tragic drama began to unfold that brought more pain to every musician in the Symphony than anyone could ever imagine.

In the latter part of 2000, our music director, Hans Vonk, began to walk differently. Something was happening to him that no one seemed to understand. Month by month his appearance changed. The maestro was, in fact, slowly becoming paralyzed. It was possibly an aftereffect of a disease called Guillain-Barré syndrome (GBS), which he had conquered years earlier. To this day, I am not sure if we all agreed on what was affecting him. Hans would not give up, however, and even after he had reached a point where he had to be assisted on and off the stage, and his conducting motions were becoming increasingly restricted, he continued to lead us in inspiring performances. Everyone in the orchestra was praying and pulling for him. When the maestro could barely direct us with physical motion, many leaders of the various sections would try to support him by moving their bodies or bows in a manner that would help lead those sitting behind them.

Eventually the moment came that all of us feared. Hans, while struggling to lead us during one of our concerts, began moving very slowly and then stopped. Little by little the musicians ceased playing. The hall was quiet. Very slowly he came down from the podium and was helped off the stage. I don't think that there was a dry eye or an unbowed head in our orchestra.

It was not long after this, in 2002, that our conductor made the decision to resign his post for the good of the orchestra. He wanted to confirm, with all his heart, how hard it was for him to leave us. I feel that it was so painful for him to leave because, when he was conducting us and making that great music, he was lifted above the horror of his circumstances. By retiring, he sacrificed his own comfort for our benefit.

Now the Saint Louis Symphony was, for the first time in its history, without a conductor. We knew the search would soon begin to fill the vacancy. Where was it to end? No one knew, but we all were sure that whoever joined us would be great. We had just lost a great man, and we somehow had to attract another great man to lead us. We would have had it no other way.

CHAPTER

64

THE SEARCH BEGINS

With the announcement of Maestro Vonk's resignation, we soon learned that Itzhak Perlman was going to be our interim conductor, with the title of Music Advisor. Well, that was kind of a surprise. Everyone knew that he was one of the world's greatest living violinists, but could he conduct?

It turned out that he could. Perhaps more important, he brought to us more than just some good baton technique. Itzhak is an amazing musician, and he shared his musical concepts with us. That was a joy. One was always impressed with how he was able to draw such beautiful music from his violin. Now we were able to witness how he arrived at those marvelous interpretations because, in effect, we had become his violin. He stroked us as if we were his Stradivarius, very lovingly. I think we returned the warmth. Besides sharing his brilliant musical ideas with us, he demonstrated something more important—courage. He showed us that if you have a dream, a beautiful vision, you may have to develop courage to realize it.

Itzhak has a physical challenge. He used crutches to get to the podium. Once the performance was over, he had to grab those crutches from the high chair he'd been conducting from and maneuver off the podium down to the stage. The skill he demonstrated in accomplishing this act could not be matched by the best Olympic athletes. It was at these moments that we all realized what the word "courage" meant.

Itzhak not only had to conduct many of our rehearsals and concerts during his two years with us as our interim conductor, he also had to play an important role in the audition process. He was a very important member of the Symphony's audition committee. Now it was the finalists in the violin auditions who needed courage. After they had made it past the preliminary auditions, which were held behind a giant screen on the stage of our concert hall, they had the pleasure of finally seeing, at their final test, who their most important critic was. Suppose you where trying out for the Yankees, and you saw that Joe DiMaggio was one of your judges. Get the picture?

CHAPTER

65

I GOTTA STAY ONE MORE YEAR

Originally I had planned to retire from orchestra playing in 2004. After playing principal cello in the Saint Louis Symphony for thirty-six years, I was looking for a change. I had a lovely condo on the side of Mt. Werner in Steamboat Springs, Colorado. The thought of skiing all winter was beckoning me.

Then came David Robertson. In the year 2004, which I thought was to be my last with the Symphony, David Robertson was named as our new music director. He worked with us quite a lot at that time and, wow, did he impress me. I thought, "He will be here next year, so maybe I should postpone my retirement one more year." Sure, there are times when playing in a great orchestra is boring. There are times when you secretly glance at the clock, trying not to let the conductor notice your shallow behavior. Or if the clock has been removed from the stage, you can always use the brushing-your-forehead-with-your-hand-with-the-wristwatch-on-the-wrist technique. I didn't do that too often. Occasionally, when I had two hundred seventy measures rest, or the music had a really boring cello part, or the conductor was less than inspiring, the job almost became work. When David Robertson got up in front of us, however, he led us with his brilliant, dancing conducting style, his incredible aphorisms, his detailed descriptions of particular scenes in literature that he wanted us to duplicate, his humility, and his love for everything on and coming from our stage in Powell Hall. It was a no-brainer. I decided that I had to stay one more year and experience what he was offering. I never regretted my decision.

My last season, which ended in 2005, was one of the most enjoyable years of music making that I have ever had. Robertson really impressed me: The Brahms and Beethoven symphonies that he did were stupendous. There were many other incredible moments that I experienced during my last season.

On November 7, 2009, five years after I had retired from the Saint Louis Symphony, I made my annual trip back to St. Louis. As usual, when visiting my old hometown, I went to hear my old hometown symphony. The concert that evening was the most thrilling of all the concerts that I have seen or heard David Robertson conduct. As the glorious sounds of the orchestra soared up to my seat in the balcony, tears filled my eyes. Was I hearing the music of Brahms, Beethoven, or Wagner? No, I was looking down on one hundred of my former colleagues and friends as they performed a whole evening of music by America's new George Gershwin.

I bet you have guessed who it is. You're right, it was the music of John Williams, the great composer of movie scores (remember *Star Wars*?). Why did I feel so moved? So many things came together as I heard the music flying up to me. Well, one reason was that, for many years, I had been feeling alone in my admiration for the music of John Williams. It hadn't seemed as though we "serious" musicians took him seriously. But that evening, everyone did. The orchestra and David Robertson presented the audience with one of the most vibrant performances I had ever heard in Powell Hall. That got to me.

David Robertson used a unique approach that evening. He did not allow the audience to know which famous film scores, from the hundreds that John Williams has composed, were to be performed. Robertson announced each piece just before performing it. His talking to the audience made the evening that much more captivating.

It might be worth noting here that I asked at least a dozen people in the audience if they were regular symphony goers, and they said no. From what I could tell, most people in the audience were first-timers. Then I asked some of them if they'd consider coming to some other concerts after hearing the music that evening. "Oh, yes!" they assured me.

Seeing so many people in the audience who were touched by the magnificent music of a composer I have always loved, and having the music pour forth from my old friends and former colleagues on the stage of Powell Hall, did it. If you had been in my shoes, don't you think you might have shed a tear or two?

66

WHERE ARE THEY GOING? UP!

In the thirty-seven years that I lived with the Symphony, I witnessed incredible efforts made by the musicians, our staff, the board, our donors, the community, local journalists, business leaders, and others that brought the SLSO to where it is today. Though there were incredible struggles along the way, I must say that I enjoyed being along for the ride. I have mentioned only a few of these struggles in this book.

There were at least five strikes, one or two lockouts (the latest in the first two months of 2005), the death, in 2007, of one of our finest music directors, Hans Vonk, and the death, in January 2009, of one of our most brilliant executive directors, Randy Adams, who was a key person in making the Symphony financially stable. I also remember that, in my early years before Randy, we had to cope with a wicked revolving door on the sixth floor of Powell Hall, through which seven or eight executive directors entered and exited like speeding trains. That was not easy for us.

Everyone, including those who might have been with us only for a short time, made contributions that enabled the orchestra to make it through its financially gloomy time. Through it all, there seemed to be a wonderful spirit that would not leave us. "You must continue to share your music with the world" seemed to echo from every corner of our concert hall. "Let nothing stop you from doing this" was the end of the message. I think we all listened.

In the year 2009, all the orchestras in the country had to cope with the terrible downturn in the economy. This was damaging to most of them. The president of the Kennedy Center, Michael Kaiser, who has been described as one of the wisest art administrators in the country, posted an article, on November 9, 2009, in *The Huffington Post,* titled "Does the Symphonic Orchestra Model Work?" He says, "Somehow the cost structure for American orchestras has risen to the point that every orchestra is likely to struggle to make ends meet." Wow!

On top of that, in the September 2009 edition of *Senza Sordino,* the official publication of the International Conference of Symphony and Opera Musicians, there were many articles addressing the challenges facing orchestra musicians throughout the country. But wait, there's more.

In the same edition, an address by ICSOM's chairperson, Bruce Ridge, to the International

Executive Board, included this statement: "Despite the crisis that has occurred in this year of need, some orchestras continue to make advancements." Then he specifically named three. You guessed it. The Saint Louis Symphony was one of them. See, all that work, by all those who had gone before, paid off.

Of course, many who were involved with the efforts that brought the orchestra to where it is now will tell you, "It wasn't easy." In the end, it was the teamwork, the dedication, and the sacrifices made by all that resolved the financial challenge. The incredible leadership exhibited by so many at different times has enabled the Symphony to be one of the few orchestras in the country that appears to be moving forward in so many ways.

The Symphony has been unbelievably fortunate in getting just the right person, at just the right time, to fill its important leadership positions, which, often tragically, become vacant. For example, I think that, with the new president and executive director, Fred Bronstein, the SLSO has acquired a "leader for our time." I won't bore you with the details. If you want to be as impressed as I am, Google him. Then you will see why I'm betting on the Saint Louis Symphony.

Oh, that's right. I forgot, they also have David Robertson and one hundred whiz kids.

CHAPTER

67

RETIRE? REALLY?

Writing this book has been both pleasurable and painful. The pleasurable aspect leads me to urge everyone to write a memoir. The Symphony's former principal flutist, Jacob Berg, commented, "If everyone took your advice, John, the world would soon be filled with paper." He was right, but there are so many interesting stories out there to be told that I would put up with that. A twelve-year-old cello student of mine, George Huestis, told me, "Writing releases emotions and that's good." George has already begun his memoirs.

Writing has released my emotions. It's helped me appreciate all the good things that have happened in my life. I have many friends who have blessed my journey along the way.

The Saint Louis Symphony has been a giant limousine for a major part of my joyride. My traveling companions as well as those numerous friends in the audience cheering on the

Symphony have given me much happiness. Often when I walked out onstage just before a concert and looked into the faces of our audience members, I could swear that I knew them all. They looked so familiar that I thought I was seeing my next-door neighbors. Some had been listening to me and my fellow musicians, once a week, for over thirty-seven years. We always smiled at each other over the stage lights, nodding with a friendly greeting before we dove into the pleasant task at hand.

We had the opportunity on the stage to show off to our friends the magnificent music that we had worked so hard on all week. Those in the audience got to sit there comfortably, to share in our recent discoveries, and to listen to the stories that the music told.

Purists would argue that there are no stories in non-program music. I don't agree. My proof of this is in the faces of some of the less inhibited orchestra musicians, who show with their expressions exactly what the composer meant emotionally in every little melody or rhythmic motif. Their faces will mirror the composer's feelings, sometimes two hundred years after they were set down on paper. Joy, fear, peace, sadness, determination, and more—it's all there. There is even a plot to the story as you hear the composer move determinedly from sadness to joy and then, finally, to peace. If you still don't believe me, try picking out two enthusiastic players sitting close to each other and see if they don't have similar body movements and facial expressions as they perform.

The Saint Louis Symphony has an abundance of these enthusiastic musicians in its midst, and that is one of the reasons it's so special. One has to be careful because every orchestra musician probably thinks that his symphony is the special one. I know I do. Maybe you would agree with me if I had the time and space to tell you about each orchestra member. There is so much more to tell: This book is just the tip of the iceberg.

Now to the sad part: Writing this book has reminded me that I have not been on that wonderful stage with all my friends since I retired in 2005. I stopped going to those rehearsals on Tuesday mornings, when we got our first taste of the music for the week; when we got to hear what new insights our maestro had learned about Bruckner's *Symphony No. 5*; when we saw all our colleagues, or should I say "family," again after a day or two of boring rest, playing tennis or doing errands.

None of this concerns you, however, because even though I am gone from the Symphony now, I have left a part of me in Powell Hall, just as Henry, Leonard, Tom, Walter, Marilyn, and those hundreds of others before me have. More important, if you do come, your presence will make you, too, a part of our great legacy. This is all the more reason why you should attend the Symphony.

All major cities have great orchestras whose members have hundreds of stories to tell, as well as a few Beethoven symphonies to perform. If you adopt a member of your symphony, he or she will fill you in on every humorous moment in its history. So, go! Leave the TV. Take the kids. Maybe they will fall in love with some masterpiece as I fell in love with Handel's *Water Music* some sixty years ago. Bring your binoculars, though, because you will need them to pick out some player who is about to get off track as I did occasionally. Symphonies, sometimes, are even more fun to watch than to hear.

Things are changing. I know that symphonies and their leaders, including the Saint Louis Symphony, are looking into many ways to build audiences. They have to. They want to please you. Because we are now living in a very visual time, some audiences, both now and in the future, will expect more than sound. Perhaps symphonies can add some form of visuals, such as a giant screen providing close-ups of the musicians and the conductor. Don't forget, concert halls are not as small as they were in Haydn's day. A little more technology will probably reintroduce intimacy to our large, modern auditoriums. Who knows? Even a wonderful restaurant in the concert hall would be an advantage.

Orchestras need you. We all need each other, and without you, orchestras get that empty feeling. Keeping this need for each other in mind, I leave you with just one thought. Could you really enjoy a *Star Wars* movie without a fine orchestra like the Saint Louis Symphony making that great John Williams's score come alive? Be honest. All right, turn off the sound, and then you'll see the point I'm making. Similarly, could a vibrant city and its citizens express its vibrancy without its symphony? The city would have no inspiring sound. In fact, I couldn't imagine a world without symphonic music. It's what I did. It was my life. It was my community. How am I ever going to stop playing in an orchestra?

CHAPTER

68

CODA

After my retirement from the Saint Louis Symphony in 2005, I became a ski bum in Steamboat Springs, Colorado. I had a ball. My condo was on the side of Mt. Werner; I could ski out my sliding glass door down to the ski lift. During the first year of my retirement, I was on my skis every day for three or four hours. "Gee," I thought, "maybe I could manage to survive without playing in an orchestra." After all, I had recently joined with two marvelous musicians, Judy Lynn Stillman, a pianist, and Dmitri Pogorelov, a violinist, to form a trio called The Generations Trio.

I also joined the local Steamboat String Quartet with Teresa, Bonnie, and Mary Ann. It is so much fun. We play all over town. My friend Gary Sheldon, Principal Guest Conductor of the San Francisco Ballet, also invites me to his festivals, where I was blessed to meet Judy and Dmitri. I even started an arts seminar in Steamboat Springs for adults, called Arts for the Soul. I have a lot going on. Did I really need to be playing in an orchestra as well?

Within a year I broke down. I joined the local Steamboat Springs Orchestra, conducted by my old friend Ernest Richardson.

Now I ski only once a week.

Oh, and by the way, I think the concert counter is now at 10,121 and counting.

o   o   o